ROSIE

ROSIE

Essays in Honour of Rosanna 'Rosie' Hackett (1893–1976):
Revolutionary and Trade Unionist

Mary McAuliffe
editor

ARLEN
HOUSE

ROSIE

is published in 2015 by
ARLEN HOUSE
42 Grange Abbey Road
Baldoyle
Dublin 13
Ireland
Phone/Fax: 353 86 8207617
Email: arlenhouse@gmail.com

Distributed internationally by
SYRACUSE UNIVERSITY PRESS
621 Skytop Road, Suite 110
Syracuse, NY 13244–5290
Phone: 315–443–5534/Fax: 315–443–5545
Email: supress@syr.edu

978–1–85132–142–1, paperback

Typesetting by Arlen House

CONTENTS

For Rosie
and all the women activists
of the Irish Women Workers' Union
and the Irish Citizen Army

Catherine Ann Cullen

NAMING A BRIDGE
for Rosie Hackett, the first woman honoured in a Dublin bridge

To make a bridge, you first must see the gap,
then fling yourself full-length across the space
like Rosie Hackett did for sixty years:
the factory girl who did not know her place.

Ah, Rosie knew that place and all its wrongs:
the sixty-hour week on the factory floor,
the union badge that barred you from your work,
the strike turned back upon the locked out poor.

Her life's three struggles forged one steely frame:
the fight for women, workers, and the Plough.
she raised a rebel banner from a roof,
for workers' holidays, she raised a row.

A name so nearly lost, now set in stone:
to name this bridge reclaims her for her own.

Mary McAuliffe

INTRODUCTION

Any snapshot of Irish women's history from the mid-19th to the early 20th century will demonstrate that many women were active in the fields of nationalism, socialism, feminism, politics, the arts and culture. However, research has shown that Irish society was slow to accept female participation in public activities, be they cultural, educational or political. In 1881 when society was questioning the suitability of female participation in formal education, the Ladies' Land League was taking a lead role in the battle for tenants' rights. In the 1890s and the early decades of the 20th century when women's role outside the home was a contested idea, many Irish women took, very successfully, to the public domain to protest their right to a political, social and cultural voice. Irish women's involvement in nationalism, the Easter Rising (1916), the War of Independence (1919–1921) and the Civil War (1922–1923), in trade unionism, in the Dublin Lockout (1913), in the ongoing campaigns for workers' rights, in feminism and the fight for women's rights, are all areas which have received significant attention from historians in the past three decades. From general surveys to biographies and autobiographies the history of women's involvement in this period is perhaps the fullest we have for any period of Irish history. However, while there has been an increase in published histories dealing with women's contribution to much of the 19th and 20th century, we still have a serious lack of public commemoration of women's roles. This fact is most incongruous given that this is our decade of commemoration (1912–1923) and we now know so much more of the vital part women have played in our recent histories. Ubiquitous images of men in most of our commemorative spaces serves to lessen the significance of the contribution of all women. The gendered naming of public spaces and structures embodies the continuing exclusion of the histories and memories of women.

While there are a few structures, spaces and statues which commemorate women in the landscape there is an absence of any trace of women's contribution to Irish history. Where, we must ask, are the grand monuments (statues, roads, railway stations) to our female patriots, our female politicians, our female trade unionists, our female writers and artists? On the main street of our capital city we have statues to several noted leaders: Daniel O'Connell, the Liberator, justly celebrated for his contribution to Irish politics, especially his achievement of Catholic Emancipation; James Larkin for his contribution to trade unionism and working-class rights; Charles Stewart Parnell for his contribution to Home Rule and the Land League. But where are the statues to Delia Larkin who was also a champion of workers' rights, especially women workers; where is any plaque to Anna Parnell, sister of Charles, and founder of the Ladies' Land League? We could commemorate, in towns and streets throughout the country, any number of members of Cumann na mBan, or the Irish Women's Franchise League, the Irish Citizen Army or Inghinidhe na hÉireann to name but a few organisations in which women were active. We now know the histories of many of our women politicians, writers, revolutionaries and religious which begs the question, is their contribution lesser because of their gender? This decade of commemorations gives the public and the state the opportunity to correct this commemorative imbalance.

In 2013 the newest bridge over the River Liffey in Dublin was named the Rosie Hackett Bridge. This is the only bridge along the course of the Liffey which is named after a woman and indeed one of the few public structures in Ireland named for a woman. In 2012 the Commemorative Naming Committee, a sub-committee of Dublin City Council, publically advertised for suggestions for the name of the new bridge. Previously Liffey bridges have been names after famous Irish writers, James Joyce, Samuel Beckett, Seán O'Casey, or politicians, Isaac Butt, Daniel O'Connell, Henry Grattan, as well as male revolutionaries and rebels such as Jeremiah O'Donovan Rossa, Liam Mellows, Rory O'Moore, Seán Heuston, as well as one named for the temperance campaigner, Fr Theobald Mathew. When the call for names was announced many groups and individuals responded and dozens of names were suggested, among them quite a few women, including Abbey actors Maire Allgood, and Siobhan McKenna, writers Maeve Binchy, Lady Gregory and Patricia Lynch, 1913 Lockout activist Alicia Brady (killed by a stray bullet during that strike), revolutionaries Countess Markievicz and Elizabeth O'Farrell, artist Eileen Grey, civil rights campaigner, Dr Sarah Clarke, Gaelic leader and 16th century West of Ireland 'pirate queen', Grace O'Malley, sportswoman Kay Mills, as well as a suggestion that the bridge be named the Magdalen Laundries Bridge to commemorate the women who were incarcerated in the Magdalen Laundries. Among the early suggestions one name stood out, that of trade union activist, revolutionary and campaigner for the rights of working women, Rosie Hackett. An effective social media campaign, a series of public lectures and op-eds in the print media soon brought Hackett to the attention of the general population. A shortlist was produced in which Hackett was included. When the list of the final five names was announced it included writer Bram Stoker, activist Willie Birmingham, Legion of Mary founder, Frank Duff, sportswoman Kay Mills and Rosie Hackett. A vote taken by Dublin City councillors saw Hackett win with 192 votes, and the other woman shortlisted, Kay Mills, in second place with 176 votes. On 2 September 2013, the Council declared that the new bridge over the River Liffey was going to be named the Rosie Hackett Bridge. In honour of that naming this collection of essays serves to commemorate the life's work of Rosie Hackett and several of her female contemporaries who were active in the nationalist, trade union and feminist movements of the early to mid-20th century.

Angelina Cox, Lisa Connell and Jeni Gartland

THE ROSIE HACKETT BRIDGE CAMPAIGN:
THE REDISCOVERY OF A FORGOTTEN HISTORY

The bridges arching over the River Liffey memorialise cherished historical and cultural figures; the Butt Bridge, named after Isaac Butt, the founder of the Home Rule movement in Ireland; the Grattan Bridge, named after Henry Grattan, the 18th century Irish politician and orator, the Sean O'Casey Bridge, named after the dramatist and writer, and the Fr Mathew Bridge, named after Fr Theobold Mathew, the 19th century priest and temperance reformer. Every bridge in Dublin city centre is named after an important historical or cultural figure and, prior to the successful Rosie Hackett Bridge Campaign, every bridge in Dublin city centre was named after a man. In 2013 Dublin city council began tendering for proposals to name the bridge which was under construction near Marlborough Street in Dublin's city centre. A campaign was mounted to name the new bridge in honour of trade unionist and 1916 veteran, Rosie Hackett. The following describes the story behind that successful campaign.

MOTIVATION BEHIND THE CAMPAIGN

The motivation behind the Rosie Hackett Bridge Campaign emanated from the absence of proper recognition for the contribution and sacrifice rendered by women in the social and political struggles of modern Ireland. The standard Irish history lesson describes the bravery of a handful of men and the odd maverick woman in bringing about social change. The constant urge to commemorate these few well-known names self-fulfils the standard narrative, while writing brave women, like Rosie, out of history. This trend of non-recognition is mirrored in women's under-representation in politics and many other public forums. The lack of role models for young women is a significant factor contributing to women's reluctance to compete for public office. The practice of naming streets, bridges and other landmarks after cherished historical and cultural figures is an important form of recognition for their contributions. Lamentably, however, women's contributions to historic struggles for independence, the trade union movement, the arts and culture have failed to receive interpretation in Dublin city's landscape. The Rosie Hackett Bridge pioneers endeavoured to redress the gender imbalance which was projected in the architecture and infrastructure of Dublin city centre. It struck us that on the occasion of constructing a new bridge a timely opportunity was an opportune moment to address this gender imbalance in the architecture and street names of Dublin city centre. Therefore, the campaign aimed to resurrect the forgotten story of an ordinary woman provoked into action by extraordinary circumstances.

ROSIE – A GOOD FIT

This central motivation underlying our campaign required proposing a historical figure to represent the typical woman whose story has largely been written out of history. After extensive research and consultation with historians and members of Dublin City Council, the name and history of Rosie Hackett was suggested. Having read more into her story, she seemed to be the ideal figure around whom to base our campaign. Thus, the campaign did not begin as a concerted effort to name a bridge after Rosie particularly. Instead, Rosie represented the spirit of our campaign and her story embodies the strife and struggle expended by the countless women whose lives, activities and sacrifices have never been recognised in the tapestry of Irish social history. Just as the majority of Dublin City Council came to support Rosie, as the campaign progressed we became captivated by Rosie's story; her humble working-class roots, her defiant and unrelenting sense of justice and her undaunted struggle for her vision of a more equal and just society. We became dedicated to commemorating and celebrating her life's work in the trade unions and her role fighting with the Citizen's Army in the 1916 Rising. We took inspiration from her story and in some ways it was possible to relate Rosie's fight to the situation faced by young people in Ireland today. The battleground between labour and employers today is drawn around issues such as youth unemployment, precarious work, unpaid internships and zero-hour contracts. As young activists, we aim to honour Rosie's memory by campaigning against poor working conditions for young people and settle the unfinished business that the activists of the 1913 Strike and Lockout fought for.

The campaign proper began when we contacted all the councillors on Dublin City Council to canvass their support for the idea of naming the bridge after Rosie Hackett. We corresponded with the councillors over email and telephone, outlining the case for naming the bridge after Rosie. Replies from some very enthusiastic councillors encouraged us to pursue the campaign further and continue to work on achieving a broad-based support for the Rosie Hackett Bridge Campaign. With the help of Labour Women Chair, Sinéad Ahern and Dublin City Councillor Andrew Montague, we arranged a meeting with the labour group on the council, who at this point had committed to supporting the campaign to name the bridge after party founder James Connolly. However, we received a very positive reaction from most of the Labour group at this meeting. They seemed convinced by the need to recognise and pay due regard to the whole range of historic figures in the Labour tradition.

The Labour Movement, in particular, has a proud and bountiful tradition of activism. We have an exceptional record in recognising and celebrating our historic leaders; James Connolly, 'Big' Jim Larkin, and Tom Johnson are rightly regarded as among our most prominent historical figures. However, constantly relying on those few men to tell the historic story of the Labour Movement only tells part of our story. Recognising and paying due regard to the whole range of historic figures in the Labour tradition, as this campaign did, only serves to further enhance the historic prestige enjoyed by the Labour Movement.

CAMPAIGN STRATEGY

Engaging with the media constituted a key component to raising the campaign's profile. Establishing Rosie's story in the minds of the relevant stakeholders was achieved by writing articles about Rosie and the campaign. We were successful in having them published in a number of print media and online journals including, the *Irish Times*, the *Irish Left Review*, the Journal.ie, as well as appearing on RTÉ interviews and numerous radio interviews. Our campaign provoked some indignant backlash from other campaigners with some healthy debate ensuing over what name the bridge should bear, serving to highlight further our campaign to name it after Rosie. We also worked on promoting the campaign through social media. Our Rosie

Facebook page was a very effective means to advertise aspects of the campaign, including sharing Rosie's story and advertising public events in relation to the campaign.

On foot of recognition gained through our media strategy, we received pledges of support for the campaign from a number of interested parties, most notably from the Irish Women Workers' Union (IWWU) commemoration group. Through collaborative efforts with the IWWU commemoration group, the campaign really gained momentum. We arranged regular meetings with representatives from this group, whose historical expertise, enthusiasm and encouragement had the effect of energising the campaign in the weeks prior to the conclusion of the Council's deliberations on the matter.

Together we compiled a lengthy list of high-profile supporters, arranged to have an opinion piece on the Rosie Hackett Bridge campaign published in the *Irish Times*, and organised a public meeting, in Liberty Hall, to inform the public and attract attention to our campaign. There was a very well-attended public meeting that night, consisting of representatives from Dublin City Council, the trade union movement, Labour Youth and members of the general public. We benefited greatly from the wit and skill of able comedian Tara Flynn who entertained us as MC for the night. We learned about the social and economic context of Rosie's early life, trade union and revolutionary activities from historian Dr Mary McAuliffe and gained an insight into Rosie's later life from her nephew John Gray, who provided us with amusing anecdotes from his memories of his elderly aunt, noting that Rosie's spark and social awareness remained with her into old age.

Shortly after the success of that event, the campaign culminated with Dublin City Council voting to name the new bridge after Rosie Hackett, thus establishing the *Rosie Hackett Bridge* as the first bridge in Dublin city centre to be named after a working-class woman. Representatives from the Rosie Hackett Bridge campaign, from Labour Women and Rosie's nephew, John, sat in the public gallery in City Hall to watch the voting procedures and ultimately to hear the Lord Mayor christen the bridge – *The Rosie Hackett*.

The procedure for voting on the naming of the bridge went as follows. There were five candidates on a shortlist including the old age campaigner and founder of A.L.O.N.E., Willie Bermingham, the founder of the Legion of Mary, Frank Duff, All-Ireland medal winning Dublin camogie player, Kay Mills, writer and author of *Dracula*, Bram Stoker and, of course, revolutionary and trade union activist, Rosie Hackett. Councillors could allocate a number between one and five to each candidate, representing the number of votes they wished to cast for a particular name. The votes were simply counted up and with fifty-one councillors voting, Rosie Hackett finished with a convincing one hundred and ninety two points. The first runner-up, being Kay Mills, finished with one hundred and seventy six points, followed by Willie Bermingham, Bram Stoker and Frank Duff respectively. It was heartening and, hopefully, an indication of Dublin City Council's acknowledgment of the need to redress the gender balance in street and bridge names that the only other woman on the shortlist came second in the councillors' votes.

CONCLUSION

Reflecting on the progression of the campaign, it is clear that the combination of starting with a good idea and the skill and dedication of the people involved, as well as support from Dublin City Council, most notably Councillors Dermot Lacey and Andrew Montague resulted in our success. The Rosie Hackett Bridge Campaign consisting of Jeni Gartland, Lisa Connell, Angelina Cox, Billie Sparks, Therese Caherty and Emmet Malone, with help from a wide range of individuals, who were proud to work together to make a bit of history and pay due homage to Rosie Hackett. The bridge opened in May 2014. It is hoped that Rosie's memory will serve as a testament to the struggles hard fought and won, and an important reminder of the battles still raging, such as struggles against unemployment and emigration. It is further hoped that our successful campaign is just the start of a wider agenda to properly commemorate the forgotten stories of ordinary people's struggles and sacrifices for social change.

Padraig Yeates

JACOB'S FACTORY, THE IWWU AND THE LOCKOUT

The Jacob's workers included the largest single group of women locked out in 1913. They would pay a high price for their militancy and their display of solidarity with their male colleagues. The opening of W & R Jacob's cake and biscuit factory in 1853 was an important event in the social and economic development of Dublin. The Act of Union, 1801, had destroyed much manufacturing in the city, wiping out the old Protestant aristocracy of labour in the process. The new biscuit factory in Bishop's Street was erected on the site of an empty coach building works. Hours were long and basic pay low, but there was no shortage of recruits when the principal alternative employment outlets for women were domestic service, charring, dealing and prostitution. The Jacobs were Quakers and took their social responsibilities seriously. The work's handbook, *Welfare and Industry,* published in March 1913, stated that:

> One of the most essential elements in the successful
> development of a business lies in the character and efficiency
> of the workers in it, and that tells in the long run.
> To secure this efficiency it is necessary to see that the work is
> carried out under proper conditions, and in wholesome
> surroundings, and that the health of each individual is
> properly cared for. Welfare work in factories is, therefore, a
> sound business proposition independent of the other benefits
> that it incurs.

The company gave preference to 'girls' aged 15 to 25 when recruiting new employees. The Welfare Secretary was a 'Lady' who examined each applicant with the assistance of a 'Lady Superintendent of Departments' with regard 'to cleanliness, physique, condition of teeth and education'.

Enquiries were made to ascertain the applicant's 'character and family circumstances'. Once employed 'a careful record' was kept 'as to their ability, conduct etc'. There was a medical service. Visits to the doctor cost 2d and the Welfare Secretary, who was a trained nurse, attended all consultations involving female employees. The company was particularly concerned to monitor and eliminate infectious diseases. Industrial accidents were treated on site, there was a rest room and an Assistant Welfare Secretary, another 'lady', visited employees' homes to advise on public hygiene and related issues. A dental service was introduced in 1907. There was a subsidised canteen with nutritious meals, a roof garden, gymnasium, baths and a forty-foot swimming pool. There were evening classes in sewing, a choral society and drilling club for 'girls'. Men had their own gymnastic club, a total abstinence society and were encouraged to attend St John's Ambulance Brigade first aid classes. When a 'girl' left to be married she received a free wedding cake, provided she had at least three years' service. No married women were employed except widows.

It was reverberations of the 'great unrest' in Britain that disturbed this paternalistic nirvana. In 1910 the number of British workers on strike soared to half a million, to a million in 1911 and 1.46 million in 1912. Pent-up militancy was fuelled by inflation, greater legal protections for unions, introduced by a Liberal government fearful of growing electoral support for Labour and a new syndicalist-socialist gospel that inspired tens of thousands of trade union activists. Trade union leader Jim Larkin had been preaching this gospel in Dublin since 1908 and, in 1911, members of his Irish Transport and General Workers Union (ITGWU) took sympathetic strike action in support of British railway workers. The militant mood quickly spread and found echoes in some unexpected quarters. One was a school strike in north inner city area of East Wall[1] and another was a news boys' strike. The latter wanted a bigger commission than the two pennies a dozen they received from Eason and newspapers such as the *Irish Independent* and *Freeman's Journal*.[2] Larkin's *Irish Worker* provided commission of a half penny per copy.

The news boys had friends among the boy labourers in Jacob's and the latter joined the fray, no doubt inspired by the prospect of an unpaid holiday from the drudgery of the factory floor and the prospect of excitement on the picket line. By that evening, 21 August 1911, about 350 men and women from the bake house had joined the strike.[3] The next morning the entire workforce was out in sympathy. Riots broke out around the factory, stones were thrown at the police, arrests made, fines and prison sentences imposed, in short, the full panoply of industrial warfare was deployed on both sides. The same day saw bayonet charges in the South Wales coalfields and Liverpool in the throes of a general strike.[4] Jim Larkin now appeared in the unlikely guise of peacemaker. Jacob's management immediately agreed to meet and overnight the ITGWU was recognised in Bishop Street. The following week the *Irish Worker* began what became a regular 'Women Workers' Column'[5] by Delia Larkin, Big Jim's sister. On Tuesday 5 September 1911, the Irish Women Workers' Union (IWWU) was launched at the Antient Concert Rooms.[6] It was the foundation of what was to become Ireland's largest union for women workers although at this stage in its history it functioned as little more than a branch of the ITGWU. Superficially the situation would be almost identical in 1913 but why did things turn out so differently?

WHAT WENT WRONG?

In the two years from August 1911 to 1913 the ITGWU consolidated its position amongst the 1,060 male employees of Jacob's but the IWWU appears to have been less successful. Between the 1911 strike and the 1913 lockout Jacob's, with over 2,000 women workers appears to have been neglected. There was just one 'Women Workers' Column' in the *Irish Worker* devoted to the firm[7] compared with many reports devoted to much smaller employments such as Keogh's Sacks, the Pembroke Laundry and Savoy Chocolates. Once the Lockout began the Column quickly focussed on Bishop Street but by then it was too late. Attacks on strike breakers, or 'scabs', would prove counter-productive when the 'scabs' comprised the vast majority of the female workforce. The other difference of course is that George Jacob, the managing director who had been only too willing to meet Larkin in August 1911 because he was totally unprepared for the explosion of workplace militancy, was ready for confrontation in August 1913.

The fragile peace in the city on which hopes of a conciliation board were based that summer was shattered by the Dublin United Tramway strike on 26 August. William Martin Murphy, chairman of the company and president of the Dublin Chamber of Commerce locked out his workers. On Saturday 30 August Richard Shackleton sent a consignment of flour from his mill in Leixlip to his fellow Quaker George Jacob in Bishop's Street, having already locked out employees who were members of the ITGWU. When the flour arrived at Jacob's ITGWU members refused to unload it. They were dismissed. On the same day notices banning the ITGWU's Red Hand badge on the premises appeared, effectively the union was being de-recognised.[8] Later on Saturday rioting erupted across the city culminating next day in Bloody Sunday. Some 168 people were arrested, almost all of them manual workers and union activists. There were only eight women arrested, none of them factory hands, in these clashes.[9] The atmosphere was tense on Monday morning when people reported for work at Bishop Street. 670 or the 1,060 men stayed out in support of their dismissed colleagues but only 303 of the 2,085 women.

Among them was of course Rosanna (Rosie) Hackett, employee number 169.[10] She was one of 176 Bake House female operatives who stayed out, compared with 108 who went to work. In every other section of the factory the vast majority of women passed the pickets. At this point in time we can only speculate on the reasons for the different responses to Jacob's offensive. As the name suggests the Bake House was the production centre in the plant and working conditions were amongst the worst in the factory. It was also the area of greatest interaction between women and their more highly unionised male colleagues. Average rates of pay in the Bake House were relatively high at 8s 2d for a 54-hour week. But the capacity to earn more was limited because there was no access to piecework. Rosie Hackett was on a slightly higher rate of 9s and sometimes worked up to six hours overtime a week, but it netted her less than 1s extra in her pay packet. Basic pay could be as low as 4s in other departments but piece work could yield a weekly income of up to 14s.[11] George Jacob correctly calculated there would not be a repeat of the dramatic 1911 show of solidarity. He brought a small number of male employees over from the company's Liverpool factory to perform essential tasks, recruited new 'girls' locally and, by 15 September, he had the Bake House back in production. The same day the company advertised in the newspapers for men and boys, followed on 3 October with a call for more 'girls'.

Strikers were given until 15 October to return or be crossed off the books. A loyalty bonus was introduced for employees passing the pickets of 2s a week for men and 1s for women. This followed close on the heels of the employers' formal rejection of proposals to end the Lockout by the Board of Trade mediator Sir George Askwith. A total of 43 women returned by the deadline but only 12 appear to have done so early enough to secure loyalty bonuses. Daily notices were then placed in the newspapers seeking new recruits until 3 November. That day saw the most serious disturbances around Jacob's since the riots at the start of the Lockout. There were violent clashes between mass pickets and strike breakers. One incident involved 16-year-old Mary Ellen Murphy, who received a month's imprisonment for boxing the ears of another girl and calling her a 'scab'. The case aroused indignation because, the women's prison being full, she was sent to High Park Convent where it was feared she would be incarcerated with 'fallen women' in the Magdalen Laundry there. James Connolly denounced the move and, when the nuns assured the public that Murphy had been kept away from their other charges he was accused of anti-clericalism.[12] The 'fallen women' were recruited on both sides as another weapon in the class war. Once the Christmas trade finished Jacob's had no need of recruits until March, at which point strikers could apply for vacancies. They were subjected to the full rigour of the vetting process, including a full medical examination before being rejected. Thus Dublin's most paternalistic employer provided one of the Lockout's most ruthless demonstrations of victimisation.

NOTES

1   http://1913committee.ie/blog/?p=370#more-370.
2   *Irish Worker*, 26 August 1913.
3   George Jacob in Evidence to the Askwith Tribunal, 2 October 1913, *Irish Times*, *Irish Independent* and *Freeman's Journal*, 23 August 1911. The *Irish Times* report says 4,500 workers struck in Jacob's but this was impossible as the company employed less than 3,200. The report seems to conflate figures for all the workers in dispute in the city that day.
4   The best recent summary of the 'great unrest' in 1911 is *Historical Studies in Industrial Relations* No 22, 2012. For the Irish dimension see Francis Devine's essay, 'The Irish Transport and General Workers Union and Labour Unrest in Ireland, 1911'.
5   *Irish Worker*, 2 September 1913.
6   Mary Jones, *Those Obstreperous Lassies: A History of the Irish Women Workers' Union* (Dublin, 1988), p. 1.
7   *Irish Worker*, 9 September 1912.
8   Patricia McCaffrey, 'Jacob's Women Workers During the 1913 Lockout', *Saothar 16* (Dublin, 1991). Padraig Yeates, *Lockout: Dublin 1913* (Dublin, 2000), p. 152.
9   *DMP Prisoners* Book 1911–1913, pp 227–236. Private Collection.
10 *Jacob's Wages Books* National Archives, Four Courts Accession No 1072/1/30 20–35.
11 *Jacob's Wages Books* National Archives, Four Courts Accession No 1072/1/30 20–35.
12 Peter Murray, 'A Militant Among the Magdalenes: Mary Ellen Murphy's Incarceration in High Park Convent During the 1913 Lockout', *Saothar 20* (Dublin 1995).

James Curry

Jennie Shanahan and the Irish Women Workers' Union

When Jane 'Jennie' Shanahan passed away in late 1936 she was remembered by Cathal O'Shannon in *Labour News* as 'one of the brightest and most popular of Dublin's working-class women' during the early decades of the twentieth century, 'as loyal and true and brave a fighter as the working-class movement ever bred'.[1] In the Dublin-based weekly labour paper's next issue Louie Bennett remembered Shanahan as 'a good comrade', one who 'never sought notoriety, nor even claimed the position in her own world to which her character and talents entitled her', content as she was to quietly 'serve the causes she loved in obscurity'.[2] As this second description suggests, the woman to whom both were referring, 'a worker and a fighter for Labour in every field in which Labour was called to battle', to again quote O'Shannon, has largely been forgotten in the mists of time since her passing.[3]

Jane Shanahan was born on 24 March 1891 at her South Dublin tenement family home, 52 Dolphin's Barn Lane, the sole daughter among four surviving children from the marriage of Westmeath-born bricklayer's labourer Michael Shanahan and his Wicklow-born wife Margaret (née Clancy). Her two eldest brothers, William and Patrick Joseph, would become bricklayer's labourers like their father, an occupation known colloquially in Dublin as being a 'hoxie'.[4] Among five other siblings to pass away during infancy was an elder sister named Catherine, who was born on 11 March 1878 shortly after their parents' marriage. All of the family were Roman Catholic in their faith. In the 1911 national census Shanahan, popularly known as 'Jennie' or its old Dublin vernacular pronunciation 'Jinny', was occupationally recorded as a cook and domestic servant. She was living at the time with two brothers and their parents in a second-class private dwelling house at 2.2 Dawson Court, in the Royal Exchange Ward near St Stephen's Green. A decade earlier the entire family had been recorded living with a widowed boarder in a first-class tenement house at 41.2 Upper Mercer Street, located in the nearby Mansion House district.

At some point after April 1911 Shanahan, like many young Dublin women of a similar background, obtained employment at Jacob's Biscuit Factory on Bishop Street, only to lose her position during the 1913–14 Dublin strike and lockout. She was presumably a member of the IWWU, which had been launched by James Larkin in early September 1911 and initially led for almost four years by his sister Delia. Cathal O'Shannon claimed that Shanahan sacrificed her job at Jacob's 'willingly and gladly', and for a period 'assisted Countess Markievicz in the Liberty Hall soup kitchen set up to feed starving locked-out workers' and their families.[5] After joining the Irish Citizen Army upon its formation in November 1913 (without taking a military rank due to her sex), Shanahan went on to be appointed as the manageress of a women workers co-op at

31 Eden Quay by James Connolly. This co-op specialised in producing men's working shirts featuring the Red Hand badge crest of the Irish Transport and General Workers' Union (ITGWU), which sold for 2s. 6d. In a November 1936 reference supporting her pursuing of a government military pension, Helena Molony revealed that in 1915–16 Shanahan 'was in charge of the premises 31 Eden Quay, which was a constant meeting place for the Provisional Government, and in which was a printing press, used extensively for Govt. purposes'. She also revealed that 'to a large extent', the command of the women's section of the Irish Citizen Army was in Shanahan's hands during this period, with her taking part 'in all the Army manoeuvres' and helping 'in the training of recruits'.[6] Parodying the simile 'a wolf in sheep's clothing', Molony described the co-op as 'a tigress in kitten's fur', revealing that in addition to all its other revolutionary activity, 31 Eden Quay 'also served as a receiving depot for small parcels of arms and ammunition'.[7] In the two weeks prior to the Easter Rising Molony and Shanahan would often sleep at night on a pile of men's overcoats in a room behind the co-op shop, including on Easter Sunday, a day of 'confusion, excitement and disappointment' at Liberty Hall following Eoin MacNeill's famous Irish Volunteers countermanding order in the *Sunday Independent*.[8]

The following day the pair were among the small 'nest of rebels who defied authority at its gates',[9] setting out for Dublin Castle as part of Commandant Seán Connolly's small Irish Citizen Army contingent of approximately 20 men and women that seized City Hall. After being arrested late that same night, Shanahan was among those released from Kilmainham Jail on 8 May, the day of Michael Mallin's execution by firing squad. Irish Volunteer leaders Eamonn Ceannt, Seán Heuston and Con Colbert were also executed that morning, but it was Irish Citizen Army man Mallin's shooting which stuck in Shanahan's memory when she later recalled the timing of her release.[10] Shanahan continued to serve with the Irish Citizen Army in the aftermath of the Rising proving herself 'a willing worker for the Republican cause' who was always 'ready for any work at a moment's notice'.[11] She took part in the War of Independence and Civil War, as well as carrying out various other 'activities in defence of the Republic' up until 1923.[12]

In his *Labour News* obituary tribute to Shanahan, Cathal O'Shannon particularly drew attention to the contribution which she made to the IWWU following the Rising:

> By none, I am sure, will she be more missed than by the Irish Women Workers' Union. If I am not mistaken, she gave it of her best qualities when it was being built up after her release in 1916 and may be reckoned among the pioneers. And I am sure that her influence, her help, her counsel and her never-ending patience and industry have done more for trade unionism among Dublin women workers than any but the very few will ever realise. She was one of the finest type of Dublin's women workers and Irish trade unionists, and the girls and women of her class may feel deep pride in her.[13]

Louie Bennett responded to O'Shannon's 'very moving appreciation' by confirming, in a letter to the paper, Shanahan's importance in helping to reorganise the IWWU in late 1916. Bennett recalled how she had first come into contact with Shanahan in 1915, when she and Helena Molony, in the aftermath of Delia Larkin's temporary departure from Ireland, sought help in 'trying to hold together the remnant of the old IWWU'. After holding discussions with the pair and James Connolly, however, Bennett saw 'no hope of establishing so innocent an organisation as a Trade Union' while simultaneously making and selling shirts 'symbolic of revolutionary purposes', and opted against giving any assistance. Following the Rising, with Connolly dead and Molony in Aylsbury Jail, Bennett abandoned her former reluctance and agreed to now reorganise the moribund IWWU on professional lines. Bennett would lead the IWWU for the next four decades, and in her 1937 *Labour News* letter wished to place on record the 'vital part' that Shanahan had played at the outset of her union career in late 1916:

> I was approached by Tom Foran and Jennie Shanahan and asked to make an effort to organise the women in the printing trades, who were then working under scandalous conditions – a 52-hour week with wages ranging from 5/ to 12/ a week. I knew nothing whatever about Trade Unionism, except what I had learned as a spectator of the 1913 strike, but Jennie shouldered the responsibility of instructing me … It was decided that Liberty Hall would not prove attractive to printers, so the D.T.P.S. lent us a room at 5 Lower Gardiner Street, as a meeting place on Monday evenings. Foran gave us a bundle of leaflets calling upon the women to organise, and we bought a 2d. exercise book with a red paper cover (though red, had no significance for us then) to serve as a ledger. Thus equipped, we started on our campaign. For a series of Monday evenings, Jennie and I sat in that big room waiting to enrol members, and rejoicing if contributions at the end of the evening exceeded a shilling or so. Jennie was back on the shirts then, but during the week, in obedience to her instructions, I waited at factory doors and handed out the leaflets to hostile or derisive groups of workers. It was some weeks before success began to reward us. We had our trials, but also we had a lot of fun together … I, like many others, have cause to be glad to have known her.[14]

Not long afterwards, Bennett would be somewhat contentiously involved in Shanahan finding new employment. On 8 May 1919 it was brought to the attention of the IWWU's executive committee that she had been instrumental in the recent appointment of a new forewoman at Wm. & M. Taylor's Tobacco Company, 119–121 Francis Street.[15] Although the woman's name was repeatedly given in the IWWU's handwritten executive minutes as 'Miss Shanaghan', it seems clear that this person was Jennie Shanahan, who would be occupationally listed as a forewoman on her 1936 death certificate, and have her funeral attended by employees from Taylor's, who also sent a memorial wreath. Her initial appointment with the firm, however, one of Dublin's three largest tobacco manufacturers, had not gone down well in 1919. The IWWU's executive committee were told that the fact she 'had no previous experience in the Tobacco Trade' and was an 'outsider' had greatly angered the staff at Taylor's who felt that the position should have gone to one of their own, in particular an employee with fourteen years' service.

There was also anger at IWWU committee level over the matter with one member questioning Bennett about the appointment at a union meeting on 19 June. An indignant Bennett insisted that she had acted in a 'personal capacity, and not as Sec of the I.W.W.U.', and therefore no member of the committee had any right to question her over the matter. To support this stance, Bennett explained that she had been contacted by the manager of Taylor's and asked to recommend somebody suitable for the position, since the 'one girl who would be fit for the appointment' on his payroll was not his most experienced, and there would thus be 'discontent and dissatisfaction' on the factory floor were she to be promoted from within. Bennett recommended that he hire 'Miss Shanaghan, whom she knew to be a capable worker', and refused to discuss the matter any further with the committee.

Bennett must have had total faith in the abilities and character of Shanahan, whose contribution to the re-organisation of the IWWU on an official footing is contemporaneously confirmed by the announcement, made in the *Dublin Saturday Post* on 3 February 1917, that she was elected as one of the union's two new honorary treasurers.[16] There is also her (non-speaking) attendance as one of four IWWU delegates at the annual meeting of the ITUC in early August 1921, when she was listed as living at 48 Charlemont Mall.[17] She appeared as an executive committee member of the union in the October 1919 minutes as 'Shanaghan, 27 Charlemont Mall', and from 1924 onwards as 'Miss Shanahan, 7 Eustace Street'. In February 1926 she chaired the IWWU's Annual Convention meeting, as well as presiding over the following year's morning session. At the May Day 1931 Annual Convention, representing Taylor's, she was elected as an executive committee member for the union's 'Other Industries' section. The following year this would be tweaked to the 'General Workers' section of the union. Shanahan was still listed as an IWWU executive committee member as late as 1935–36, by which point she had moved to 71 Larkfield Grove, Kimmage, with her father and younger brother Thomas.

By doing so she became a neighbour of Helena Molony and fellow Irish Citizen Army rank-and-file stalwart Maeve Cavanagh MacDowell, who both lived on the same street. All three houses, which came with accompanying small gardens, were leased from a 'Commercial Public Utility Society'.[18] These societies played a key role in the Dublin housing boom of the 1920s and 1930s, building houses for the private market in close co-operation with Dublin Corporation, who provided assistance in the form of site development and access to various grants and incentives in an effort to share the workload of rectifying a crisis in the city's housing provision.[19] The timing of Shanahan's move is likely connected to the fact that the 1932 Housing Act ensured the term 'public utility society' could refer to any registered 'society, friendly society or trade union' that had an interest in 'the erection of houses for the working classes'.[20]

Shanahan would not be a Kimmage resident for long. At the age of just forty-five, she died while a patient at Mercer's Hospital near St Stephen's Green. Her passing occurred on 29 December 1936, the same day that her sworn statement for a military pension was finally checked, with the cause of death recorded as 'Chronic neuritis Uraemia', a painful form of kidney failure.[21] A meeting of the Old Irish Citizen Army Comrades' Association was adjourned later that evening as a mark of respect to her memory. On 7 January 1937 Helena Molony revealed in a letter to the Military Pensions Board that although her friend and neighbour had been 'in failing health for some years', her death had come 'quite unexpectedly'.[22] Earlier that week Cathal O'Shannon publicly disclosed that although Shanahan had indeed suffered from 'indifferent health' for some time, most of her friends and trade union comrades were unaware 'of any illness of hers until the bad, sad news of her death in Mercer's Hospital was passed along by her intimate colleagues in the Irish Women Workers' Union'.[23] Shanahan's funeral took place on the morning of Thursday 31 December at Glasnevin Cemetery, following Mass at St Paul's Retreat, Mount Argus. Her coffin was draped in the Starry Plough flag of the Irish Citizen Army, with the graveside oration delivered by Molony, who paid tribute 'to Miss Shanahan's work in the Labour and National movements, and spoke of the trust that had been placed in her by the 1916 leaders'. At the first IWWU committee meeting held following her passing, a vote of condolence was passed for Shanahan's relatives, with members of the executive and union staff 'joined in expressions of loss and sympathy'.[24] The union's official annual report later that year opened with a short notice mourning 'the death of one of our oldest and most valued members'.

Shanahan's legacy? She was described as 'one of the founders of the IWWU, an ardent and self-sacrificing supporter of the Labour Movement and a devoted daughter and sister'.[25]

NOTES
1   *Labour News*, 2 January 1937.

2   *Ibid.*, 9 January 1937.

3   *Ibid.*, 2 January 1937.

4   *Ibid.*, p. 137.

5   *Labour News*, 2 January 1937.

6   Jane Shanahan, Military Service Pension File REF10154 (Military Archives), p. 23.

7   *Irish Times*, 23 April 1956.

8   *Ibid.*

9   R.M. Fox, *The History of the Irish Citizen Army* (Belfast, 2013 edition), p. 134.

10 Shanahan, Pension file REF10154, p. 31.

11 *Ibid.*, pp 25–26.

12 *Ibid.*, p. 23.

13 *Labour News*, 2 January 1937.

14 *Labour News*, 9 January 1937.

15 IWWU executive minutes, 8 May 1919 (Irish Labour History Society Archives).

16 Quoted in Mary Jones, *These obstreperous lassies; A History of the IWWU (Dublin, 1988),* p. 24.

17 Irish Labour Party & Trade Union Congress Official Report (1921) (National Archives), p. 223. I am indebted to Leah Hunnewell for this reference.

18 Valuation Office, Co. Borough of Dublin, Rathmines West Ward, Vol. 3 (1929–39) and Vol. 3 (1939–47).

19 See Ruth McManus, 'Public Utility Societies, Dublin Corporation and the Development of Dublin, 1920–1940' (http://staff.spd.dcu.ie/mcmanusr/Urban%20Course/documents /PublicUtilitySocietiesCorporationDublinIG29_1.pdf) (15/08/14).

20 *Ibid.*, p. 28.

21 Shanahan, Pension file REFE2338, p. 24.

22 Shanahan, Pension file REF10154, p. 29.

23 *Labour News*, 2 January 1937.

24 IWWU Executive Minutes, 7 January 1937 (Irish Labour History Society Archives).

25 IWWU Twentieth Annual Report, 1936–37 (Irish Labour History Society Archives).

Francis Devine

WORKING IN A ROSE GARDEN RATHER THAN FISHING SHED:
JACOB'S & THE IRISH WOMEN WORKERS' UNION,
1911–1913

Although some male staff belonged to craft unions, the
unionisation of women in Jacob's Biscuit Factory began in
August 1911. Initially, relations between George Jacob and
James Larkin, Irish Transport & General Workers' Union
(ITGWU) and later the Irish Women Workers' Union
(IWWU), appeared peaceable. Things quickly deteriorated.
Jacob became a significant, committed ally of William
Martin Murphy in the Dublin Employer's Federation
(DEF) determination to smash the ITGWU in the 1913
Lockout.

JACOB'S BISCUIT FACTORY
In September 1913, Patricia McCaffrey identified 2,085
women workers in Jacob's. Men and women worked a
five-and-a-half hour day, fifty hour week, mostly on piece
work. Two thirds of the women had average earnings of
between seven to ten shillings a week. Male labourers

average earnings were estimated to be between fifteen to twenty-five shillings, although craftsmen's and general builders' labourers could earn over forty shillings. Craftsmen such as painters, carpenters and plumbers earned over seventy-five shillings. Women's wages were generally much lower. Examination of sweated wages in the linen and allied trades in the North of Ireland by the *Irish Citizen* in 1913 exposed wages as low as 'only a halfpenny an hour'. In comparison, according to Yeates, fourteen year old 'beginners' in Jacob's 'were in a workers' nirvana' on four shillings a week.[1] Conditions in Jacob's were difficult with petty rules and repressive discipline. In 1911, George N. Jacob, aged 46, lived at 731 Temple Road, Rathmines & Rathgar East, with his wife, Mary and their two children. Family status is indicated by four servants.[2] Jacob, described as Church of Ireland, was renowned as a Quaker. In keeping with that tradition, he prided himself as a paternalistic employer. Welfare provisions included a doctor and dentist in attendance at the works, canteen and recreation facilities, a roof garden, and beds for convalescent workers in the Berwick Home, Rathfarnham. Low wages meant life for many was day-to-day. The ITGWU's arrival in 1909 brought hope and expectation that things could change.[3] In 1911, a W. & R. Jacob's & Co. Ltd. Employees' Trade Union (W&RJETU) was registered, perhaps an attempt by Jacob to forestall ITGWU incursion by creating a 'house' union. The W&RJETU made no returns to the Registrar of Friendly Societies; its registration was cancelled in 1915. A W. & R. Jacob's & Co. Ltd. Girls' Sick Club registered as a Friendly Society in 1908, dissolving in 1912.[4] Guinness employed a Private Detective to provide intelligence on the ITGWU and Jacob's surely kept an equivalent vigilance regarding the perceived threat of Larkinism.[5] Whatever efforts Jacob made, they were unsuccessful as ITGWU Red Hand badges appeared on workers' lapels.

On 19 August, the ITGWU weekly *Irish Worker* announced the creation of the IWWU. Mary Jones suggests 3,000 women came out on 22 August, their actions central to the new union. Delia Larkin's impassioned rallying call identified Dublin's women's workplaces:

> Sisters ... in the mill, the factory, biscuit or jam, sack or packing – whether you are a weaver, spinner, washer, ironer, labeller, box-maker, sack-mender, jam-packer, biscuit-maker – whatever you are or wherever you work, join the IWWU.

It was formally launched on 5 September. Jacob's women were its most significant force. Delia described the IWWU as ITGWU 'affiliated' but it was separately affiliated to the Irish Trade Union Congress. Little more is made of the 1911 strike.[6] On 22 August, 'some of the boys' in Jacob's 'influenced by the newsboys, went out'. Women went out in sympathy with them or in pursuit of their own grievances. Jim Larkin effected a settlement and, according to Jacob, told him:

> 'I think you have been hardly treated. I don't approve of what has been done'. Larkin felt Jacob's were committed to revising wages. The walk out jeopardised this. A union handbill reminded staff of 'the deep necessity on your part of carrying out the agreement'.[7]

On returning to work, they should 'work together in a spirit of comradeship' with 'no recriminations, no offensive language'. Those who did cause 'any friction' would act 'the traitor and be worse than a blackleg', receiving 'no sympathy or assistance' from the union. The 'union' is not specified on the handbill but it was signed by ITGWU officials Larkin, Bohen [sic] and Burke.[8] An advance of two shillings for men and one shilling for women was agreed on 27 August, although Jacob declined to concede union recognition. The shilling differential on gender grounds was unquestioned. Had matters rested there, Jacob's relationship with ITGWU/IWWU might have remained 'normal'.[9] After the strike, the *Irish Worker* began 'a vituperative campaign' against Jacob. He was ridiculed for 'purporting to run the business for love' and 'keeping the factory open to find work for the poor'. The paper claimed that of thirteen Foremen, only one was Catholic, and he an Under Foreman; management were 'notoriously severe and dictatorial'; and the atmosphere was like a penitentiary. When girls got married, Jacob presented them with an 'Authorised Version' of the *Bible*. Larkin insisted conditions were 'sending them [the women] from this earth twenty years before their time'.[10]

JACOB'S & THE 1913 LOCKOUT

On May Day 1913, 'small but representative' ranks of IWWU women marched in Dublin 'for the first time'. Jacob's women became a conspicuous presence at demonstrations throughout the Lockout. Large contingents attended the funerals of Bloody Sunday martyrs James Byrne and James Nolan, and fellow-Jacob's striker Eugene Salmon, killed heroically attempting to rescue siblings from the Church Street tenement collapse on 2 September. William Partridge said Salmon was sacked by Jacob's 'who paid such miserable wages as compelled the poor lad to reside in the pile that was not a home but a tomb'. He concluded, 'Before God, Jacob, had killed this lad'. Jacob's had locked out staff the day before the collapse.[11] On 6 September, the *Irish Worker*, under a heading 'Tyranny in Dublin', said that on Monday morning, 1 September, three girls wearing the Red Hand badge 'were approached by Jacob's tool, Miss Luke, and told to remove their badges'. When they refused, they were dismissed. Over 250 others refused and by the end of the day, 310 women were sacked. The ITGWU began blacking Jacob's products at wharf and railhead. In fact, a notice was displayed on Saturday 30 August prohibiting wearing of the Red Hand. Three men were dismissed that day for refusing to handle

Shackleton's 'black' flour. On Monday 'hundreds of women workers failed to report for work' and 'some who did refused to remove their union badge'. Jacob's declared a lockout, interestingly three days in advance of the general DEF lockout imposed on 3 September. Jacob told the *Irish Times* he would not re-open 'until the company had sufficient applications from workers pledged not to belong' to the ITGWU, language identical to that of the infamous DEF 'document'.[12]

In another incident, Jacob's sacked ITGWU Branch Secretary Gibson, allegedly found in a public house when supposedly at work. The Branch Office was at 77 Aungier Street, adjacent to Jacob's. Jacob, a teetoller, like Larkin, told the *Irish Times*, in classic free labour speak, that he had 'no objection' to staff being in a union 'conducted on ordinary lines' but 'must in future refuse' employment to those in the ITGWU which was 'conducted with so much tyranny and injustice'. He claimed most staff came in 'as normal' but set about advertising for strike-breakers. When replacement labour arrived, it occasioned picketing and sporadic violence in Bishop Street.[13] IWWU members in Jacob's were now absolutely committed to the Larkinite cause. In Delia Larkin's *Irish Worker* 'Women Workers' Column', Jacob's featured regularly. Indeed, the dispute gave the IWWU a 'new lease of life': 'technically independent but in reality a Section of the ITGWU, it had become almost moribund by 1913'. Just before the lockout, the IWWU's 'recruitment drive had faltered', membership was down to 600 and finances were poor.[14]

STRIKEBREAKING IN JACOB'S

McCaffrey recorded 303 women 'went out' on 1 September, with 1,777 staying in. She provides a breakdown, department by department, of the 13.9% of staff who 'went out'. By 14 October, 1,441 women were at work compared to 2,085 on 2 September, suggesting that more women had refused to pass pickets, not least as, by mid-October, many strike-breakers were employed. Whatever their individual sentiments, many women, most of whom were young, would have been strongly influenced by parental attitude to their actions. The girls' wages, no more than for thousands of working-class homes, were crucial to family incomes. Decisions to forego them took courage and strong motivation. Jacob's re-opened the Bakehouse, which they need not have closed as they had sufficient staff, and by 11 October public notices suggested they had a full work complement. Anyone not returning by 15 October, and proving acceptable to management, was 'crossed off the books'. This threat had little effect. By then, any girls going to return, or not going out in the first place, had done so. Jacob's advertised again between 16 October and 3 November. The strike-breakers' arrival occasioned numerous outbreaks of disorder and, on 4 November, sixteen-year-old Mary Ellen Murphy was sentenced to a month's imprisonment for giving a young strike-breaker 'a box in the face and calling her a "scab"'.[15] Such incidents impacted on Jacob's which placed further advertisements in 'Situations Vacant' looking for 'respectable girls' in packaging and labelling. 'Industrious workers' could earn 'good wages', although no rates were quoted.[16] By January, Jacob's workforce was 'normal' and many new recruits were hired at cheaper rates. Jacob's were among the last to 'settle' matters after the Lockout. As the majority of women, 1,777 out of 2,085 stayed in, and few subsequently came out to join them, only a minority heroically fought the good fight.

Mary Neal in the British suffragist paper *Votes for Women* thought that 'so long as the girls only wore the general badge' of men's unions, the 'masters took very little notice'.[17] Employers had 'always depended on the women' to break men's strikes by working for lower wages, 'so that as soon as the women began to organise themselves, form their own Union, and wear their own badges', Jacob's took repressive action. James Connolly's 'observant eye' in the Scottish socialist paper *Forward*, 'contrasted the poverty of women's circumstances with the strength of their solidarity': 'they march out with pinched faces, threadbare clothes, and miserable footgear, but with high hopes, undaunted spirit, and glorious resolve shining out of their eyes'. The courage of Jacob's women, collectively and individually within their homes, in taking their stand, cannot be underestimated.[18]

AFTERMATH

Yeates categorised Jacob's among the 'particularly objectionable employers' and George Jacob demonstrated steely resolve to see the Lockout to whatever gruesome conclusion if it smashed the ITGWU. Jacob's claimed their wages 'compared very favourably' with those of similar employments in England and, after the Lockout petered, invited churchmen, politicians, Poor Law Guardians, 'even the Royal College of Physicians' and press to investigate conditions in Bishop Street. The *Freeman's Journal* and *Irish Independent* carried images of contented, industrious workers. The *Irish Catholic* was 'particularly enthusiastic' describing a 'Hive of Work and Happiness'. They showed a packed canteen, women dancing on the roof garden and doing gymnastics, and Total Abstinence Society men playing bagatelle in a recreation room. Their correspondent had witnessed factories from Iceland to Cairo and placed Jacob's at the 'rose garden' rather than 'fishing shed' end of the spectrum.[19] In fact, hours were reduced from fifty five to fifty for men and, from 14 October, 'loyalty money' given to those who returned to work, one shilling for women, two shillings for men. It was paid to 1,311 staff, 60.3% of the total. Jacob's refused to take hundreds back, damning their actions. Greaves states that even those taken back were 'carefully selected' and 'submitted ... to humiliating medical examinations accompanied by scornful comments'. He claimed that only 100 out of 672 men and boys were taken back and wage reductions of between two and four shillings were imposed. Women and girls 'on the whole fared better'.[20] In May 1914, in correspondence with the ITGWU solicitors rather than directly with the union, Jacob said he would 're-employ the girls of good character when vacancies occurred'. Those like Rosie Hackett and Lily Kempson were never considered to 'be of good character'.[21] Taking no further chances, Jacob's created supine house unions. On 12 February 1914 the Dublin Biscuit Operatives' Labour Union & Benefit Society (DBOLU&BS) was registered, 308T, followed on 18 February 1916, by the Dublin Guild of Female Biscuit Operatives (DGFBO), 315T. These bodies stayed in existence until the 1970s when absorbed into the Amalgamated Transport & General Workers' Union. By then the Workers' Union of Ireland also had members in Jacob's.[22] The striking women, and men, of Jacob's displayed resolve against significant economic, social and physical odds to sustain their belief in trade union rights. Unable to convince all their fellow women to join them, their battle was lost. They had struck a blow, however, and for pioneer women, like Rosie Hackett, it was central to their political formation. All Jacob's strikers, overwhelmingly anonymous, merit respect from those today facing similar organisational challenges and workplace gender discrimination.

NOTES

1 Patricia McCaffrey, 'Jacob;' women workers during the 1913 Lock-Out', *Saothar* 16, 1991, pp 118–130; Pádraig Yeates, *Lockout: Dublin 1913* (Dublin, 2000, 2013), pp xxi–xxiii, 28, 31–32, 223; Fergus A. D'Arcy, 'Wages of labourers in the Dublin building industry, 1667–1918', *Saothar* 14, 1989, pp 17–32 and 'Wages of skilled workers in the Dublin building industry, 1667–1918', *Saothar* 15, 1990, pp 19–30; Francis Devine, 'Who dared to wear the Red hand badge? Reflections of the 1913 Dublin Lockout' in

Francis Devine (ed), *A Capital in Conflict: Dublin city and the 1913 Lockout* (Dublin, 2013), pp 1–26.

2   www.census.nationalarchives.ie/reels/nai003708503/ The children were Dora, twenty, and Harold, nineteen and the servants William Williams, 32; Honoria Jordan, 32; Lucy Fanning, 27; and Mary Jane McAlister, 22.

3   William Partridge, Amalgamated Society of Engineers, Labour Councillor in Kilmainham and, by 1913, ITGWU Organiser, observed that the greatest thing Larkinism brought was 'hope' and a belief that things could be dramatically improved.

4   Francis Devine & John B. Smethurst, 'Section 2.1.2: Biscuit Makers', *Historical Directory of Trade Unions in Ireland* (forthcoming). The W&RJJETU, 292T, operated from 65 Meen Street, Dublin. The Girls' Sick Club was 1174F.

5   Patrick Coughlan & Francis Devine, 'In pursuit of Patrick Donegan, Guinness boatman, 1895–1955: a case of family history' in Francis Devine (ed), *A Capital in Conflict: Dublin City and the 1913 Lockout* (Dublin, 2013), pp 311–332.

6   *Irish Worker*, 12, 19 August; 9 September, 1911; William O'Brien, 'The ITGWU and the IWWU: a bit of history', NLI O'Brien Papers, MS 13,970; Francis Devine, *Organising History: A Centenary of SIPTU, 1909–2009* (Dublin, 2009), p. 33.

7   *Ibid.*

8   John Bohan was Secretary, No 3 Branch (High Street), see Devine, *Organising History*, p. 972; and Burke was Secretary in Bray, Shankill & Kill o' the Grange, see James Curry & Francis Devine, *'Merry May Your Xmas Be & 1913 Free From Care': The Irish Worker 1912 Christmas Number* (ILHS Saothar Studies 3, 2012), pp 25–26.

9   Cited in McCaffrey, 'Jacob;' women workers during the 1913 Lock-Out', pp 118–120; C. Desmond Greaves, *The ITGWU: The Formative Years, 1909–1923* (Dublin, 1982), p. 64.

10   Cited in Mary Jones, *These Obstreperous Lassies: A History of the IWWU* (Dublin, 1988), p. 3.

11   Devine, *Organising History, op. cit.*, pp 58–59; Chris Corlett, 'The Church Street disaster, September 1913', *History Ireland*, vol. 17, no. 2, March/April 2009.

12   Jones, *These Obstreperous Lassies* p. 10; Pádraig Yeates, *Lockout: Dublin 1913*, p. 79.

13   Yeates, *Lockout: Dublin 1913*, p. 79.

14   Yeates, *Lockout: Dublin 1913*, p. 153; Theresa Moriarty, 'Larkin and the women's movement' in Dónal Nevin (ed), *James Larkin:*

Lion of the Fold (Dublin, 1998), pp 93–101. Delia and the Liberty Players toured Britain to raise funds.

15   Peter Murray, 'A militant among the Magdalens? Mary Ellen Murphy's incarceration in High Park Convent during the 1913 Lockout', *Saothar* 20, 1995, pp 41–55.

16   Yeates, *Lockout: Dublin 1913*, p. 373.

17   Neal, 1860–1944, joined the Women's Social & Political Union in 1906 and wrote for *Votes For Women* from 1907. See *Mary Neal – an undertold story*, www.maryneal.org/index.php [accessed 16 February 2014].

18   Both cited in Moriarty, 'Larkin and the women's movement'.

19   Cited in Yeates, *Lockout: Dublin 1913,* p. 540. Jacob successfully sued the British left-leaning daily *Daily Herald* in July 1914 after they had published a less flattering view.

20   Greaves, *The ITGWU:* pp 119, 124, 126.

21   NLI, MS 27,054, correspondence William Smyth & Son with ITGWU.

22   Devine & Smethurst, *op. cit.* The DBOLU&BS operated from 15 Lauderdale Terrace, Dublin. Its membership was: 1914, 1,276; 1915, 1,500; 1920, 935; 1930, 770; 1940, 594; 1950, 496; 1960; 501; and 1964, 480. Secretary was John Hannon, 23 Nicholas Street, who was also Secretary of the DGFBO. He remained in office until 1933 and was succeeded by Francis Egan, John Kelly in 1957, and John Beatty in 1964. In the *Report of the Commission on Vocational Organisation*, 1943, the Society's written response is acknowledged and its address given as 18a Bishop Street, significantly adjacent to Jacob's Biscuit Factory. Its registration was cancelled on 14 May 1970, after the DBOLU&BS merged into the Amalgamated Transport & General Workers' Union. The DGFBO operated from 11 Lavender Terrace, New Road. Hannon was succeeded in 1933 by Ellen Gamble; 1959, Lilian Murray and 1961, Elizabeth Harwood. In 1943, the DGFBO address was Black Lion, Inchicore. Membership was: 1916, 1,255; 1930, 1,189; 1940, 1,342; 1950, 684; 1960, 826; 1970, 787; and June 1973, with 700 members, it merged with the Amalgamated Transport & General Workers' Union. It was dissolved on 19 June 1973. The Peter's Row Biscuit Operatives' Benefit Society (PRBOFS) was registered as a Friendly Society in 1899, 860F. It operated from 5 Peter's Row, Dunlin from 1913–1961 when it appears to have been dissolved.

Mary McAuliffe

ROSEANNA 'ROSIE' HACKETT:
A LIFE WELL LIVED

Sometimes what is rendered invisible by a society's historians
tells us more than we care to admit. Early twentieth-century
Ireland was dominated by politics. To read about that period
is to be persuaded into thinking that women were at home
knitting socks. Rosie Hackett could be very easily dismissed as
a newspaper vendor but when her life is examined she turns
out to have [been out] on strike ... with fellow workers across
the city during the Great Lockout of 1913.[1]

Rosie Hackett was born in Dublin, in 1893, to John Hackett,
a hairdresser and his wife Roseanna Dunne. Soon after the
birth of their second daughter Christina, in 1894, John
Hackett died, leaving the young widow in precarious
circumstances. By 1901 the family was living in a two-
roomed flat in Bolton St with Mrs Hackett's siblings John,
James and Catherine Dunne and a lodger. Like many
thousands of Dubliners the extended Hackett Dunne
family was living in a tenement. No 27 Bolton Street had
five families altogether, each family living in one or two

rooms; in total there were twenty four people sharing nine rooms. The living conditions of the poor in Dublin were among the most crowded, unhygienic and unsanitary in Europe. Reports indicted, over and again, that these tenements were 'multitudinous fever nests and death traps', owning to overcrowding, poor diet and lack of sanitation.[2] By 1914 the *Dublin Housing Inquiry Report* determined that the situation in the tenements was desperate and real solutions needed to be found. This was the Dublin in which Rosie Hackett was growing up. By 1906 her mother had re-married, to Patrick Gray, a warehouse caretaker. The family then lived in a series of rented rooms in Henrietta St, and by 1911, the Grays, Patrick and Rosanna, their sons Thomas, Patrick and Denis, along with her daughters, Rosie and Christina, and their uncle James Dunne, were living in a four-roomed house at Old Abbey St, just off Sackville St (now O'Connell St). Rosie Hackett was, by then, 17-years-old and working as a messenger in Jacob's Biscuit Factory.

Jacob's Factory was one the main employers of young working-class women in Dublin in 1911. Founded by the Quaker Jacob family in 1853, by the second decade of the 20th century the factory provided regular, secure but poorly paid employment. Activism against the exploitation of workers by George Jacob, chairman from 1901–1932 was one of the first campaigns undertaken by the trade union movement. As early as 1911 trade union leader Delia Larkin wrote that:

> Jacobs & Co. have no qualms of conscience whatever as far as the workers are concerned ... they are out to make a profit, and make it they will, even though it be at the cost of ill-health and disablement to the girls, women, and men of Dublin.[3]

Probably inspired by the conditions she found in Jacob's, even at that young age, Hackett was an active member of the newly-formed and growing trade union movement. James Larkin (brother of Delia) had set up the Irish

General and Transport Workers Union (ITGWU) in Dublin in 1909, and she was among the early members. By 1911 Larkin was furiously denouncing the pay and conditions in Jacob's, particularly the conditions endured by the biscuit makers in the bakehouse, conditions that were 'sending [the biscuit makers] from this earth twenty years before their time'.[4] On 22 August 1911, the bakehouse men went on strike for better pay. Later that day some 3,000 female employees came out on strike, among them was the young ITGWU member, Rosie Hackett. The women admitted that they were not striking for themselves but out of sympathy for the men. The years up to 1911 had been marked by strikes and industrial unrest, but for women workers, the ITGWU offered little support or protection. If the men in the bakehouse were considered badly paid, the wages of the women working in Jacobs were even worse. Of course, this was in common with women workers' wages generally; women were not seen as breadwinners or in need to a 'living wage'. Their earnings were then, and would for a long time to come, be considered secondary to the male wage in any household. When the 1911 strike was settled the men received a two schilling advance, while the women received a one schilling advance. However, Larkin helped settle the strike and, for a time, industrial peace reigned in Jacobs. This did not hold back the interest in trade unionism among the workforce however.

James Larkin had included adult suffrage and equal voting rights for women in his initial programme, but as with several of the male nationalist organisations of the time, women workers were not 'wholeheartedly welcome' in the ITGWU.[5] The plight of the woman worker was worsening, so on 5 September a meeting to formally launch the Irish Women Workers' Union (IWWU) was held in the Antient Concert Rooms on Great Brunswick St (now Pearse St). Earlier in August (the 19th) the *Irish Worker* had called for the formal recruitment of women into a women's workers union, this call was given extra impetus with the participation of the Jacob's women in the bakehouse strike on 22 August.[6] On the platform at the meeting were women activists from trade union, nationalist and feminist backgrounds. From the podium the well-known feminist and leader of the Irish Women's Franchise League, Hanna Sheehy Skeffington called on all to work together 'for the welfare of both sexes'.[7] Countess Markievicz, a member of the separatist, feminist organisation Inghinidhe na hÉireann, told the gathered women that 'as you are aware women have at present no vote, but a union such as now being formed will not alone help you obtain better wages, but will also be a means of helping you get votes'.[8] Also on the platform were the Larkins, Delia and James. Delia Larkin spoke of changing the role of women workers in Irish society, a society where women were 'weary of being white slaves who pass their lives away toiling to fill the pockets of unscrupulous employers receiving for their labours not sufficient to enable them to exist'.[9] The presence of Sheehy Skeffington and Markievicz on the platform, with the Larkins, demonstrated the strong support suffrage and separatist women gave to advancing the economic and political status of all women.

By 1911 Jacob's factory was one of the largest employers of women in the city. Many of the young women employed there, including Hackett, answered Delia Larkin's call to pay sixpence to join the IWWU.[10] The *Irish Worker* regularly complained about the treatment of women workers by Jacob's and other employers after the setting up of the IWWU. These complaints occasioned a series of strikes through 1912 and, as activist and IWWU member Helena Molony wrote, the employers began a campaign of intimidation of their women workers. They wanted to prevent their workers from joining the IWWU and even demanded that they stay away from Liberty

Hall. At this stage Liberty Hall was becoming both a social and a political hub. Some members of the IWWU became part of the Irish Workers Choir, based in Liberty Hall, and as the *Irish Worker* observed, through the choir, 'a large amount of talent was discovered among the white slaves of Dublin'.[11] Some also later became involved in the Citizen Army's Liberty Players, a dramatic group which put on plays penned by James Connolly and others; these social events helped embed the IWWU in trade union activities and networks. From these dramatic roots in the trade union revues came Abbey actors Sean Connolly and Helena Molony. The cause of labour and the cause of women were also becoming more united, as the suffrage paper, the *Irish Citizen* noted. By September 1913 'the men of Mr Larkin's union … frequently [acted] … to protect Suffragettes from the hooliganism of the Ancient Order of Hibernians – the body that is now organising the strike breakers'.[12] By the time the Lockout began in August 1913 the links between militant and radical suffrage women and labour were well advanced.

In 1913 Hackett was one of the many Jacob's workers who came out on strike during the Lockout. She wrote that as a result of the 'big strike' she became attached to Liberty Hall, and she was to remain attached for the rest of her life.[13] The Lockout began on 26 August 1913 when tram conductors pinned the Red Hand badge of the ITGWU to their lapels and abandoned their vehicles. Hackett was involved in the Lockout from the beginning and was present to hear James Larkin speak in Dublin on Sunday 30 August 1913 (Bloody Sunday). The huge crowd gathered to hear him was charged by members of the Dublin Metropolitan Police (DMP); two people were killed and over 300 injured. On that same day, 30 August, the management in Jacob's put up a notice forbidding the wearing of union badges on the premises. Later that day a delivery of flour from a mill in Lucan, which had locked out its ITGWU workers, arrived at the gate of the factory. As this flour mill was now blacklisted, members of the ITGWU in Jacob's refused to handle the delivery, in consequence, three men were dismissed from their jobs. By the next day (31 August) the situation escalated when the firemen from the bakehouse did not come in for work. By Monday 1 September, 670 men and 303 women did not turn up for work.[14] The Jacob's factory women were now engaged in the Lockout, among them IWWU member Rosie Hackett. She recalled her first day of picketing outside the factory, hearing that 'word came that the forces of law and order were on the way', news which scattered the strikers as they feared, with good reason, violence and arrest.[15] During subsequent protests a number of women strikers were arrested and one of them, Jacob's factory worker Mary Ellen Murphy, was jailed for:

> assaulting one of the girls employed by Messrs Jacob by giving her a box on the face and calling her a 'scab' on the morning of the 3rd [of Nov.], and with acting in a similar manner in the afternoon of the same day when complainant was returning from dinner.[16]

As well as taking her turns on the picket line, Hackett worked tirelessly in Liberty Hall to provide food for the families of the striking workers. Over 2,000 children from strikers' families were fed every day in this soup kitchen. There she encountered women like Helena Molony, Countess Markievicz, Kathleen Lynn, Madeleine ffrench-Mullen, Hanna Sheehy Skeffington and other members of the IWWU. Many of the suffrage women were wearing their suffrage badges as they worked alongside the IWWU women wearing their union badges. This was a space where the working women of the IWWU came in contact and got to know the radical feminist and separatist women; creating female activist networks which were to prove very vital in the coming revolution.

When the strike ended Hackett did not get her job back as she was considered a 'disruptive element'. Delia Larkin had helped set up the Women Workers Co-operative Society which aimed to provide employment for some of the 300 female strikers who had lost their jobs as a result of the Lockout.[17] This Co-op included a small shirt-making factory which employed about a dozen of the 'marked' women, including Hackett. The factory specialised in union goods, including a workman's shirt called the 'Redhand', union badges, flags and other items sold to union members. This 'workroom was opened to assist girls who had lost their employment as a result of the strike' which Hackett mentions in her BMH witness statement.[18] Apparently, because of her small stature (she was less than 5ft tall), Hackett could not use the large sewing machines but she worked where she could in the factory. She also assisted in the printing shop attached to Liberty Hall. In late 1913 a workers militia was formed as a self-defence organization for the striking workers. With the ending of the strike this Irish Citizen Army (as it became known) was re-organised in 1914 under the leadership of James Connolly. Hackett joined the women's section of the Irish Citizen Army as soon as it was formed. She wrote 'when Miss Larkin left Liberty Hall, Miss Helena Molony came to take charge, and that is when the work of the women's section of the Irish Citizen Army started in earnest'.[19] As well as her activities in both the IWWU and the Citizen Army, Hackett continued to work in the co-op shop in Liberty Hall. As well as selling the ITGWU's newspaper *Worker's Republic*, and newspapers other newsagents wouldn't stock (the *Gael, Nation, Spark*), the shop also served as a 'private post office and a receiving depot for small parcels of arms and ammunition'.[20] The activity around Liberty Hall brought the building and the shop to the attention of the authorities and Hackett was in the shop when it was raided by the Dublin Metropolitan Police on 21 March 1916. Following the publication of the

Gael newspaper's inflammatory St Patrick's Day issue, the police raided the shop. As the DMP barged in, Hackett stood her ground as, of course, she knew not only were there copies of the *Gael* in the building but there were also rifles and ammunition. 'The little girl in charge' as the *Worker's Republic* called her when reporting on the incidence, kept the police at bay until James Connolly, who had been summoned, came down brandishing a gun and told the police to 'drop those papers or I'll drop you'.[21] Subsequent to that incident a permanent guard was kept on Liberty Hall until after the Rising.

In the weeks before the Rising she attended the first aid classes organised in Liberty Hall by Dr Kathleen Lynn. From 1 April she was working with the Citizen Army members preparing haversacks, dressings and munitions. As her comrade in the Citizen Army, Bridget Brady, wrote in her pension application, the women there were making bandages, collecting cans to make bombs, making first aid outfits and taking messages when necessary.[22] The women were also gathering information and doing intelligence work. As part of her work in the shop Hackett 'worked as canvasser and traveller and was called on to carry out many confidential jobs'.[23] A week before Easter, Hackett was part of the flag-raising ceremony, when the teenager, Molly O'Reilly, was chosen by James Connolly to hoist the Citizen Army's 'Challenge Flag', a green flag with a gold harp, over Liberty Hall. She also went on Citizen Army route marches and was on the final route march on Sunday 23 April, after which she was ordered to remain, with the other Citizen Army members, in Liberty Hall until further notice. She knew something big was coming 'as some time before the Rising, Connolly told us we would have to buck up and get ready, that the day was coming'. On their final route march George Oman, the Citizen Army bugler, had sounded his bugle as they passed each of the places that were to be taken in the Rising.[24] On Easter Sunday, she was kept busy running back and forth between Connolly and the print room in Liberty Hall, with notes from Connolly containing drafts of the Proclamation. Later that night she helped deliver 2,500 copies of the final printed Proclamation to Helena Molony in the co-op shop.

On Easter Monday Hackett set off in her 'white coat … [which] was down to my heels' and had to be shortened, accompanying ffrench-Mullen, Countess Markievicz, Michael Mallin and a contingent of the Citizen Army towards St Stephen's Green.[25] Before she left she received instruction from Dr Lynn that she 'would be with Miss ffrench-Mullen. Wherever Miss ffrench-Mullen would go, I was to be next to her'.[26] When they reached St Stephen's Green, they cleared out the civilians, locked the gates and dug trenches, while Hackett helped ffrench-Mullen and several other women (including Nora O'Daly, May Moore, Bridget Murtagh and Bridget Gough) set up the first-aid station in a small lodge in the south-west corner of the Green. On Tuesday the rebels abandoned the militarily-insecure Green (they were under heavy fire from the Shelbourne Hotel) and took up positions in the Royal College of Surgeons where they remained until the surrender. Hackett was among those who made it to the College and she resumed her first aid duties with ffrench-Mullen. The College came under a sustained barrage of gunfire with Hackett coming close to death at least once. She remembered that on one occasion she:

> was lying down on one of the beds … The men were trying out some rifles they had found in the College. The people upstairs sent for me to go for a cup of tea … I had only left the bed, when a man, named Murray, casually threw himself down on it and, whatever way it happened, this bullet hit him in the face. We attended him there for the whole week. He was then brought to Vincent's Hospital where he died after a week. They remarked that had I not got up when told to go for the tea, I would have got it through the brain, judging by the way the bullet hit this man.[27]

Hackett worked in the first aid section which the women set up in the large and protected College Hall. In her recollections Nora O'Daly wrote that:

> the large blind upon which lantern slides were shown (to illustrate lectures in the College) was drawn down and that end of the lecture room was sectioned off for Red Cross work only, no one but First Aid assistants being allowed past the barrier. These consisted of Miss Rosie Hackett, Miss B. Murtagh, and myself.[28]

One of O'Daly's fondest memories from that week was of 'little Rosie Hackett of the Citizen Army, always cheerful and always willing; to see her face about the place was a tonic in itself'.[29] When the command to surrender came, delivered by Cumann na mBan member Elizabeth O'Farrell, from Pearse and Connolly, Hackett noted the deep despair that was felt by all. She saw Markievicz 'sitting on the stairs, with her head in her hands', while Mallin shook hands with all of the rebels still there, looking 'terribly pale [and] his face was drawn and haggard'.[30] Hackett was arrested along with the others, taken first to Dublin Castle, then on to Richmond Barracks, before being imprisoned in Kilmainham Jail. As they were marched away from the College, a Citizen Army captain, William Partridge, ordered Hackett and the other women around her to feel proud of their contribution. Hackett wrote that:

> Mr. Partridge was very good to us. He felt for us very much, because the crowd outside were terribly hostile. You could not imagine how they could be so terrible. He kept telling us: 'Now girls, heads erect'.[31]

She was released from Kilmainham on 8 May with most of the other female detainees.

After her release Hackett resumed her activities as a member of the Citizen Army and worked from Liberty Hall, once the Hall, which had been ruined by bombardment during the Rising, was restored. The Hall soon became a centre of activities, as Hackett noted 'when Miss Molony succeeded in getting the soup kitchen going again, it was a great cover-up, and we were able to carry on our activities, where a lot of other places were not'.[32] On the anniversary of the Rising in 1917 she was among the women who organised the re-printing of the Proclamation, copies of which were then postered up throughout the city. On the first anniversary on Connolly's death, 12 May 1917, she, Helena Molony, Jinny Shanahan and Bridget Davis hung a banner which read 'James Connolly Murdered 12th May 1916' from Liberty Hall's top parapet. As she describes the incident;

> Miss Molony called us together Jinny Shanahan, Brigid Davis and myself. Miss Molony printed a script. Getting up on the roof, she put it high up, across the top parapet. We were on top of the roof for the rest of the time it was there. We barricaded the windows. I remember there was a ton of coal in one place, and it was shoved up against the door in case they would get in. Nails were put in. They barricaded themselves in and held off a large police contingent, which had arrived to remove the banner, for several hours.[33]

Hackett claimed it took '400 police' to break down the barricade and get the banner down and thousands of people gathered across the river from Liberty Hall to see the banner.

Hackett also resumed her trade union activities. She worked with Molony, Louie Bennett and Helen Chenevix to re-organise the IWWU and was elected clerk of the IWWU. In 1918 when the ITGWU revised its rules and allowed women members she became the full-time No. 1 Branch official of the newly-formed women's section of the ITGWU. She remained a member of the Citizen Army until about 1919 when, like many of the Citizen Army women, she joined Cumann na mBan, in her case, she joined the Fairview branch. Quite a number of women left the Citizen Army in the post 1918 period. While these women were committed to the freedom of Ireland they were also dedicated trade unionists. Frank Robbins, a Citizen Army comrade found that by 1919/1920 'practically all the women who had taken part in the 1916 Insurrection were not now members of the Citizen Army' and revealed one of the reasons they left was:

> due to the fact that new members had been recruited into the women's section who had very obnoxious pasts as far as Trade Union matters were concerned; at least two of them had actually scabbed in the 1913 strike. This, of course, was too much for the women who had lost their jobs fighting to uphold Trade Unionism in the past to accept, not to mention the trials and tribulations endured in the performance of their national duty by taking part in the Easter Week Insurrection.[34]

Hackett contributed to the War of Independence as a member of Cumann na mBan. During this period her room in Liberty Hall was a central depot for messages and a safe meeting house for members of the Dublin battalions of the IRA. She narrowly escaped arrest several times as there were constant police and British army forces raids in Liberty Hall. After the truce and Treaty debates she took the pro-Treaty side during the Treaty debates, left Cumann na mBan which was mostly anti-Treaty, and was an ardent supporter of Michael Collins.

Hackett continued to work in Liberty Hall for the rest of her career, running the ITGWU's newspaper and tobacconist shop at 33 Eden Quay. May O'Brien, who worked as a clerk in Liberty Hall, remembered Hackett's warm and engaging personality, describing her as:

> a little wispy woman ... the image of the little spinster teacher in the cowboy films: small, slight, grey hair in a bun with stray bits falling to her face, wire-rimmed glasses ... and a rather prim expression.[35]

O'Brien also witnessed Hackett defending strenuously the sacrifices the women and men of 1916 had made when anyone disparaged them. In particular she describes an occasion when Hackett took on a 'big brawny man' who came into the shop and proceeded to denigrated the heroes of 1916 within her earshot, challenging him to:

> Just say again what you said about 1916. About the men and women of the Irish Citizen Army. Just mention again Connolly, a man who died to let scum like you live, you slimy slithery toad. Say that again about 1916 and I'll see you crawl back under the stone you crawled from under ... was what we went through worth it? The pain and anguish and the blood that was shed, all the sacrifices, was it all for nothing after all. Jesus Christ, did they die for nothing?[36]

She shouted at him with tears in her eyes. O'Brien said that the man was unable to put a finger on this furious 'bantam cock of a woman'. Hackett worked in the shop until 1957 when she retired. A report on the occasion of her retirement in the union's newspaper described how the:

> pint-sized, rather elderly woman locked the door of the IT&GWU Transport Tobacconist Shop on Eden Quay for the last time and in doing so wrote finis on fifty years' active association with the Irish Trades Union movement.[37]

She lived to see the new Liberty Hall rise on the footprint of the old and was a guest of honour at the official launch in May 1965. In 1970 she was presented with a gold badge by the ITGWU in recognition of her long service with the union. On that occasion the *Irish Press* described her as the 'Rose of the ITGWU'. When interviewed after the ceremony Hackett remarked that if only 'Mr Connolly were living, women not be in the backward position we are in today'.[38]

Like many of her revolutionary and trade union comrades Hackett was disappointed at the position of women in Irish society. In 1936, for instance, Helena Molony, in her opposition to the Conditions of Employment Bill (1936) which sought to restrict women's employment, was disgusted that Labour leaders were supporting a 'capitalist Minister in setting up a barrier against one set of citizens'.[39] Also opposing the Act was veteran feminist Hanna Sheehy Skeffington, who had spoken, in 1911, at the inaugural meeting of the IWWU. She noted that for women driven out of jobs:

> there was a terrible alternative such unfortunate women might take, and it would be at the door of Mr Lemass ... if women were driven to take such an alternative.[40]

These activist women, many, like Hackett, motivated by the 1916 and 1922 promises of full and equal citizenship kept fighting for the rights of the Irish woman in spite of the continuing erosion of her rights. Rosanna 'Rosie' Hackett died on 4 July 1976 and was buried in Glasnevin with full military honours. From her teenage years she dedicated her life to fighting for the rights of her class, her gender and her nation. She is deservedly commemorated in her native city, a proud working-class woman who fought for the good of all.

NOTES

1   Margaret Mac Curtain, 'The "Ordinary" Heroine; Women into History' in Margaret Mac Curtain *Ariadne's Thread; Writing Women into Irish History* (Galway: 2008), p. 217.

2   Kevin C. Kearns *Dublin Tenement Life: An Oral History of the Dublin Slums* (Dublin: 1994).

3   D. L., 'Women Worker's Column' in *Irish Worker* (21 September 1912), p. 2.

4   See Mary Jones *Those Obstreperous Lassies; A history of the Irish Women Worker's Union* (Dublin: 1988) pp 1–6.

5   See Jones *Those Obstreperous Lassies.*

6   Jones *Those Obstreperous Lassies,* pp 1–5.

7   *Ibid,* p. 1.

8   *Ibid.*

9   *Ibid,* pp 5–6.

10   On 1 September 1913, some 2,085 women were employed there. Source is Patricia McCaffrey, 'Jacob's Women Workers During the 1913 Lockout', *Saothar,* 16 (Dublin, 1991).

11   Jones *Those Obstreperous Lassies,* p. 9.

12   Donal Nevin *James Larkin; The Lion of the Fold* (Dublin; 2006), p. 94.

13 BMH WS 546 (Rosie Hackett), p. 1.
14 McCaffrey, 'Jacob's Women Workers During the 1913 Lockout' p. 122.
15 James Curry 'The Little Rose of the ITGWU' in *Crossing the Liffey in Style: Rosie Hackett Bridge* (Dublin, 2014), p. 6.
16 Peter Murray, 'A Militant Among The Magdalens? Mary Ellen Murphy's Incarceration in High Park Convent During the 1913 Lockout', in *Saothar*, 20 (1995), p. 41.
17 Senia Pašeta *Irish Nationalist Women, 1900–1918* (Cambridge: 2013), p. 126. Including Rosie Hackett, between 400–500 female strikers lost their jobs permanently as a result of the Lockout.
18 BMH WS 546, p. 1.
19 BMH WS 546, p. 1. This would have been around 1915.
20 Curry 'The Little Rose of the ITGWU', p. 7.
21 BMH WS 546, p. 2.
22 Bridget Murphy (nee Brady), Military Pension Application File, NAI: MSP34REF32618.
23 BMH 705 (Christopher Joseph Brady), p. 2.
24 BMH WS 546.
25 BMH WS 546, p. 5.
26 *Ibid.*
27 *Ibid.*
28 Nora O'Daly, 'The Women of Easter Week' in *An tOglac*, 1926, p. 5.
29 *Ibid.*
30 BMH WS 546, p. 8.
31 *Ibid*, p. 9.
32 *Ibid*, p. 10.
33 *Ibid.*
34 BMH WS 585 (Frank Robbins), p. 157.
35 May O'Brien, *Clouds on my windows: a Dublin memoir* (2004), pp 50–51.
36 *Ibid.*
37 Curry 'The Little Rose of the ITGWU', p. 11.
38 The *Irish Press*, Tuesday 1 September 1970, p. 1.
39 Cullen Owens *Louie Bennett* (Cork, 2001), pp 84–5.
40 Margaret Ward (ed) *In Their Own Voice: Women and Irish Nationalism* (Dublin, 1995), p. 183.

Gerri O'Neill

WOMEN OF THE IRISH CITIZEN ARMY: TIME FOR A REAPPRAISAL?

The established narrative of the Irish Citizen Army (ICA), and particularly of the women who served in that organisation, may require reassessment in light of the recent release of the Military Service Pensions files.[1] The documents on the ICA reveal that between 200 and 230 members participated in the 1916 Rising, more than 30 of whom were women, although there is some duplication in the list due to name changes following marriage.[2] The detailed accounts of both male and female activists contained in this collection were compiled in the early to mid-1930s, more than a decade and half before the Bureau of Military History (BMH) witness statements, on which historians based much of their understanding of the Irish Citizen Army to date. It is likely that the names of people and places and the sequence of events leading up to the Easter Rising, and beyond it, were perhaps clearer in the minds of many of the participants in the 1930s than they were in the 1950s. Furthermore, many ICA members who placed pension claims did not submit BMH witness statements; some chose not to, others were too old or too ill and some had already passed away. Consequently, the recently released pension documents are perhaps the most detailed and authoritative accounts of the turbulent 1916 period and the ICA's participation in the Easter Rising.

Unlike the Irish Volunteers and Cumann na mBan, the Irish Citizen Army, from its formation in 1913, accepted members of both sexes, although only two women, Countess Markievicz and Dr Kathleen Lynn, held rank. Both Helena Molony and Madeleine ffrench-Mullen were widely regarded as officers by the rank and file of the women's section of the ICA, and Marie Mulholland's work on Dr Kathleen Lynn states that they were 'officers trained and equipped on a par with their male counterparts'.[3] However, Helena Molony's Military Service Pension application states otherwise. She lists her rank as 'Private' during the 1916 Rising and was granted a pension at 'Rank E', that of a non-commissioned officer or private.[4] In her sworn statement to the pension advisory board, Molony explains that she, and other Citizen Army women, had made a conscious decision not to claim any rank 'for the purposes of pension'. In the section dealing with Civil War activity, she stated that she was recognised as a Captain 'on the military side', but that 'these ranks were nebulous and had not really the same significance as men's ranks'.[5] Molony was one of only a few women who remained within the ranks of the Irish Citizen Army through to the end of the Irish revolutionary period, although she worked in close liaison with both Cumann na mBan and the IRA. She documents that the ICA was the 'first army in the world where men and women were on equal terms' but clarifies this by explaining that members of the ICA were allocated positions and tasks in line with their abilities rather than their sex.[6]

Nonetheless, there was a separate women's section within the ICA whose members reported directly to the women officers and participated in first aid training in Liberty Hall under the supervision of Dr Lynn.[7] The first aid classes increased in frequency in the weeks immediately preceding the Rising and were by then attended by both sexes. Frank Robbins, a sergeant in the ICA, described the lectures as having 'a fine psychological effect in so far as they blended the men and women of the Army much closer together'.[8] This remark suggests that hitherto training for men and women had been conducted separately, although there is ample evidence to suggest that women had received small arms training from male members of the ICA and had participated in target practice at the Citizen Army's training ground at Croydon Park. Women also participated in route marches, both day and night marches, although some members of the women's section remained behind to provide 'light refreshments' for those returning from military exercises.[9]

A week before Easter 1916, a flag-hoisting ceremony was arranged by the ICA at Liberty Hall. A sixteen-year-old member of the women's section, Molly O'Reilly, was chosen by James Connolly to be the central character in this symbolic ceremony. ICA member Rosie Hackett was dispatched to the O'Reilly home to bring Molly to Liberty Hall so that Connolly could speak with her.[10] Molly gladly accepted the honour and on Palm Sunday 1916, four companies of the ICA lined up in Beresford Place in front of Liberty Hall accompanied by a Guard of Honour, buglers and drummers. The event had been well publicised and the surrounding streets were filled with Dubliners who had come to witness the ceremony. James O'Shea was on duty with the Citizen Army that day and described the sequence of events in his witness statement:

> The drums were piled and the flag was handed to Mollie (sic) O'Reilly. She unfurled the flag. The Guard presented arms,

bugles sounded and she marched guarded by a squad of men with fixed bayonets. She walked through the Guard of Honour and up straight to the flag staff on Liberty Hall.[11]

The green flag with the golden harp flew for the first time over Liberty Hall to cheers and applause while Connolly, who appeared in full military uniform for the first time, addressed the crowd. It is perhaps symbolic that Molly O'Reilly had long red hair and was dressed that day in a green skirt with a flowing train, a white blouse and a sash of green, white and orange.[12] O'Reilly epitomised the mythical Caitlín Ní Houlihan about to 'summon her children to her flag and strike for her freedom'.

At 12 noon on Easter Monday 1916, following a frantic few days preparing rations and first aid kits, O'Reilly did just that. Liberty Hall was a hive of activity from early that morning as most ICA members had spent the night there. Rosie Hackett recalled helping to provide breakfast for everybody as final preparations were made, when she was called to Dr Lynn to receive her instructions for the day.[13] Hackett was told that she would be on first aid duty in St Stephen's Green and was to report directly to Madeleine ffrench-Mullen. Hackett's friend, Brigid Davis was to accompany Dr Lynn to Dublin Castle. Both women were issued long white coats and red armbands to indicate that they were on first aid duty. Those ordered to take Dublin Castle fell in behind Seán Connolly and marched towards Dame Street; Helena Molony recalled that she led a group of nine women, while Connolly had about twenty men.[14] Molly O'Reilly was one of that small group of women. Meanwhile, Rosie Hackett was one of those who fell in behind Michael Mallin and marched towards St Stephen's Green where she and ffrench-Mullen set up their first aid post in the centre of the park.

Both groups became engaged in gunfire exchange almost immediately but Seán Connolly's group were the first to fall. Following an abortive attempt to take Dublin

Castle, in which a policeman was shot by Connolly, the group fell back to City Hall and occupied that building instead. Shortly afterwards, Connolly himself was shot by a sniper and although attended to by Kathleen Lynn, his wounds proved fatal. Lynn was then the most senior ICA member present and so assumed command. Molly O'Reilly was given a dispatch to bring to James Connolly in the GPO to advise him of events in City Hall and sent back there almost immediately with a response from Connolly instructing that the position was to be held at all costs.[15] O'Reilly moved back and forth between the two locations carrying dispatches until finally she was unable to gain access to City Hall due to the heavy fire surrounding the building. Later that evening the contingent there was forced to surrender and all surviving ICA members were taken prisoner. O'Reilly escaped arrest as she was still moving between HQ in the GPO and the various outposts under James Connolly's command.

By Monday evening, the ICA position in St Stephen's Green was also under heavy fire as British troops had taken position on the roof of the Shelbourne Hotel and were peppering the park with gunfire. When the position of the insurgents became untenable, a decision was taken to evacuate to the nearby College of Surgeons; this location was occupied by the Citizen Army on Tuesday morning and held until the surrender. ffrench-Mullen and Hackett immediately set about establishing their first aid post in a safe part of the building and began tending to the wounded. Hackett reports in her Military Service Pension application that she was 'rendering first aid and actively engaged in dressing and attending wounded members of the forces' for the duration of Easter week.[16] One of their more seriously wounded patients was Margaret Skinnider, the only female member of the ICA injured by gunfire during the Rising. She was treated by ffrench-Mullen and Hackett from Thursday of that week through to the surrender on Sunday when she was removed to the nearby St Vincent's Hospital. According to Skinnider's pension application, her wounds were incurred when 'in charge of detachment of men sent out early on the morning of 26th to destroy houses in Harcourt St to cut off enemy approaches'.[17] She had gunshot wounds to her right arm and her back that required hospitalisation until the end of June 1916.

Margaret Skinnider was a member of Cumann na mBan in Glasgow prior to the 1916 Rising, but joined up with the Irish Citizen Army for the Rising in Dublin. She subsequently returned to Cumann na mBan and remained active with them through to the end of the Civil War. However, she was not the only Cumann na mBan woman who fought with the ICA in the College of Surgeons and St Stephen's Green. Several Cumann na mBan women who had failed to mobilise with their own branches joined with the St Stephen's Green garrison or moved between there and other outposts with ammunition and dispatches. Both BMH witness statements and Military Service Pension applications indicate that there was a considerable amount of cooperation and crossover between the women of Cumann na mBan and the ICA in 1916 and beyond. In fact, the relationship between the organisations, and of the individual women who made up the membership of each, may be more nuanced than previously understood. A deeper appraisal of these relationships is now possible as a result of the wealth of documentation available to historians in the Military Service Pensions files; it is hoped that new research based on these files will be published in time for the 1916 centenary.

NOTES

1   Military Service Pensions Collection, Bureau of Military History.

2 Military Service Pensions Collection, Irish Citizen Army membership file. Unsworn statement made before the advisory committee by John O'Neill on 29 March 1935.

3 Marie Mulholland, *The Politics and Relationships of Kathleen Lynn* (Dublin, 2002), p. 35.

4 Military Service Pensions Collection, Helena Molony, Ref 11739, p. 15.

5 Military Service Pensions Collection, Sworn statement of Helena Molony, 3 July 1936, Ref 11739, p. 6.

6 Military Service Pensions Collection, Sworn statement of Helena Molony, 3 July 1936, Ref 11739, p. 3.

7 BMH WS 585 (Frank Robbins), p. 18.

8 Frank Robbins, p. 18.

9 Frank Robbins, p. 10.

10 *Irish Press*, 29 March 1937.

11 BMH WS 733, (James O'Shea), p. 34.

12 *Irish Press*, 29 March 1937.

13 BMH WS 546, (Rose Hackett) p. 5.

14 BMH WS 391, (Helena Molony) p. 33.

15 Military Service Pensions Collection, Sworn statement of Mary (Molly) Corcoran née O'Reilly, 11 December 1936, Ref 20325, p. 1.

16 Military Service Pensions Collection, Application for a Service Certificate, Rose Hackett, 3 December 1935, Ref 20787, p. 9.

17 Military Service Pensions Collection, Application for a Service Certificate, Margaret Skinnider, 28 May 1935, Ref 19910, p. 4.

Lauren Arrington

FEMALE REBELS AT THE
ROYAL COLLEGE OF SURGEONS, 1916

After a weekend of bomb-making at Liberty Hall, James Connolly took the Irish Citizen Army out for a Sunday afternoon march through Dublin's city centre. He was incensed by Eoin MacNeill's countermanding order cancelling the planned rebellion but refused to be thwarted: the IRB military council of which the Citizen Army was a part had determined that the Rising would be postponed, but for just one day. Rosie Hackett strode out behind Connolly, crossing Butt Bridge, College Green, turning down Grafton Street, and heading west along York Street by the College of Surgeons. 'As we came to each of these places', she later remembered, 'the bugle sounded. We did not know it at the time but, as each place was taken afterwards, we thoroughly understood what that route march was for'.[1] On their return to Liberty Hall, Connolly told his assembled troops that 'every man and woman, and every boy and girl, that had marched this day were now soldiers of Ireland'. One of Hackett's comrades was Margaret Skinnider, who made it clear in her autobiography, *Doing My Bit for Ireland* (1917), that first under the constitution of the Citizen Army and then under the Proclamation of the Republic, 'we had the same right to risk our lives as the men'.[2] So-called auxiliary work would prove to be no less dangerous than battling at the front lines. As the Rising began Hackett was assigned to accompany the Citizen Army's Chief Medical Officer, Madeleine ffrench-Mullen, to the first-aid post in St Stephen's Green. These women did not see themselves as non-combatants, nor were they perceived as such by the British snipers who ignored the rules of war and fixed their sights on the large red crosses that marked their bibs, but missed and instead shot up their skirts and shoe leather.[3]

At first light on Tuesday, British soldiers who had taken up positions on the roof of the Shelbourne Hotel and behind barricades on Merrion Row began firing down into the Green. The ICA retreated from their trenches, dug at Michael Mallin's imprudent instruction, into the shrubbery of the park, where they held out for an astonishing four hours. Finally, at eight o'clock in the morning, Mallin ordered their retreat into the fortress of the Royal College of Surgeons, which Constance Markievicz, Frank Robbins, and Mary Hyland and Lily Kempson of Cumann na mBan had secured the previous day.[4] By the time the cache of rifles that was rumoured to be stored there was found, the Green had been abandoned. The College would now be essential to their survival. Dodging bullets, flying gravel, and jeers from some of the city's disaffected citizenry, Hackett darted across York Street to the College, where she discovered that Markievicz and Robbins had already established a headquarters on the first floor. Beds and mattresses had been smuggled over from the Turkish Baths in order to organise the building's lecture halls into a dormitory, recreation room, dining room and sickbay. A tricolour was raised from the College's roof, to the puzzlement of one Trinity student who remarked on the strange combination of 'green, white and orange. I can't understand why it was orange, but perhaps they call it yellow!'[5] Markievicz ordered Hackett to stay indoors, which Hackett later felt was overly protective. In fact, as an assistant to Madeleine ffrench-Mullen she was essential to the College's makeshift hospital, which relied on skilled first-aiders who could make the best of the few supplies that had been plundered from neighbouring shops and houses. Other women worked as couriers and as soldiers, free to serve as they saw fit. Margaret Skinnider played both parts, donning a green moleskin uniform of knee breeches, belted coat and puttees when she took up her position as a sniper on the College's roof but changing into her plain grey dress and hat in order to travel incognito as she carried dispatches back and forth between posts.

From their new stronghold, the ICA attempted to mount a bombing campaign to set fire to the perimeter of the Green and drive back the British troops. However, the improvised weapons, 'oil-cans through the neck of which a galvanised iron tube went down', were too delicate.[6] When Skinnider struggled to push a bomb through the window of the Shelbourne, it detonated early, revealing their position to the British soldiers above who immediately fired, killing teenager Fred Ryan who was with her and wounding Skinnider in three places.[7] City Councilor William Partridge, a leader in the ICA, helped Skinnider back to the College, where she underwent a rudimentary operation, after which she lay incapacitated as the battle moved closer to the surrender. Skinnider believed that the College was 'impregnable' and that the machine-gun bullets were like 'dried peas' pelting its stonework, but the building was not as impenetrable as she thought. Once, Hackett rose from her mattress to get a fortifying cup of tea and returned to find that the man who lay down after her had been shot in the face.[8]

As the days wore on, food became a greater concern than ammunition. Amongst the College kitchen's scant provisions, Nellie Gifford found a bag of oats and made endless pots of porridge, which Markievicz later credited with keeping them going, along with weak bouillon made from the stock cubes in their provisions and biscuits smuggled over from Jacob's factory. When martial law was declared on Wednesday, communication between posts became more difficult and keeping up a strong morale was even more important. Markievicz and Mallin brought their troops together in the evenings to pray and to sing. Somehow, in the midst of the fighting, the weekly edition of the *Workers' Republic* was published; in place of the regular ICA column, it carried Markievicz's poem, 'Our Faith', exhorting comrades to fight and to die, 'Be the chances nothing at all'.[9] As the sound of the British gunboat shelling Liberty Hall reverberated through the walls of the College, Markievicz and Mallin began to prepare for a direct attack. They transferred the wounded, including Skinnider, to local hospitals, stored grenades along the staircase in preparation for a last-stand, and even began to talk about retreating into the Dublin hillsides to mount a guerrilla war.

On Sunday, word came that Pearse and Connolly had signed the surrender. Soon afterwards, Pearse's nurse, Elizabeth O'Farrell, arrived at the College in the company of British Army Major de Courcey Wheeler. Markievicz was the first to see the order since Mallin was resting upstairs. Her immediate impulse was outright refusal; it seemed better to die on the spot than to give in. Nevertheless, she woke Mallin, and after a tense conversation, they agreed to obey the instructions of their commanding officer. Astounded by the turn of events, Markievicz could only repeat the phrase, 'I trust

Connolly'.[10] Soon after, Hackett found her sitting on the stairs in the College, her head in her hands, as Mallin made the rounds shaking the hands of his comrades: 'He took my hand and did not speak. He was terribly pale'.[11] Because of her aristocratic bloodline, her piercing English accent, her statuesque presence, her political prominence, and her bold personality, Constance Markievicz became a cipher for popular hostility to the women who fought in the Rising. The national press delighted in sensationalised accounts of the evacuated College of Surgeons, describing the anatomy room, which had been converted into a crude mortuary, as a gothic tableau:

> slabs for bodies being made of old House of Lords benches removed from the Examination Hall. A rude crucifix, composed of black metal coffin breastplates, the central plate bearing the letters 'R.I.P.,' was affixed to the wall.[12]

The caretakers' quarters, 'It was here that Countess Markievicz slept', was described in extensive detail, including the remnants of the sickly sweets that had nourished the Citizen Army in the absence of proper food: 'she and the others seem to have had a partiality for chocolates'.[13] The *Daily Mail* and the *Irish Times* gave similarly theatrical accounts of Markievicz's surrender, describing her as an overgrown leprechaun, 'dressed entirely in green, including green shoes. She walked up to the officer, and, saluting, took out her revolver, which she kissed affectionately, and then handed it up'.[14] This image of Markievicz as an absurd, incongruous figure was first used to discredit the revolutionary objectives of the Rising. Later, the same iconography was used to create a cult of personality that celebrated her exceptionality as a female militant. Yet Skinnider's role as a sniper, Hyland and Kempson's part in capturing the College of Surgeons, and ffrench-Mullen and Hackett's dangerous work as medical support all show that Markievicz was not exceptional as a female combatant. At the surrender, as she and Mallin led their rank-and-file in the long walk from the College of Surgeons to Richmond Barracks, assailed by cries of 'shoot the traitors' and 'bayonet the bastards', Rosie Hackett and her comrades marched behind them.[15]

NOTES

1   Bureau of Military History, Witness Statement (BMH WS) 546 (Rosie Hackett).
2   Margaret Skinnider, *Doing My Bit for Ireland* (New York, 1917), p. 124.
3   BMH WS 585 (Frank Robbins); Skinnider, *Doing My Bit*, pp 124–25, 171.
4   Charles Townshend, *Easter 1916: the Irish Rebellion* (London, 2005), p. 168.
5   Townshend, *Easter 1916*, p. 159.
6   Countess de Markievicz, 'Women in the Fight' in Roger McHugh (ed.), *Dublin 1916: an Illustrated Anthology* (London, 1976), pp 122–125.
7   Skinnider, *Doing my Bit*, pp 147–49.
8   BMH WS 546 (Rose Hackett).
9   C. de Markievicz, 'Our Faith', *Workers' Republic*, 27 April 1916.
10   Michael T. Goy and Brian Barton, *The Easter Rising* (Stroud, 1999), pp 94–95.
11   Foy and Barton, p. 94.
12   'Inside the Royal College of Surgeons: After the Rebels Left', *Weekly Irish Times*, 20 May 1916.
13   *Ibid*.
14   'Surrender of the Countess Markievicz', *Irish Times*, 2 May 1916.
15   Foy and Barton, p. 96.

Elizabeth Gillis

'THEY PROVED THEIR WORTH':
FORGOTTEN WOMEN IN THE REVOLUTION

The year 2014 was certainly going to be the year when the
role of Irish women in the history of our country would be
finally fully recognised. From naming the new bridge
across the River Liffey after Rosie Hackett to unveiling a
plaque at Wynn's Hotel commemorating the founding of
Cumann na mBan in 1914 and a proposal to name
numerous buildings and public spaces in Cork after
women who took part in the struggle for Irish
independence nearly a century ago, this recognition is long
overdue. Irish freedom was not won by the actions of a
few, but of many. And while every movement needs its
leaders they would have nothing and would achieve little
without the support of and the willingness to act
demonstrated by the thousands of ordinary men and
women who chose to stand up and say enough is enough.
This was as true in Ireland in the years 1913–23 as it is
today. In that effort to achieve independence for Ireland
were to be found thousands of women, young and old,

who chose not to not only follow the path of domesticity, marriage and motherhood that society dictated they should follow. Instead they played a vital role in the revolutionary movement, a role recognised by many of their male comrades who recalled that, without their help and support, the revolution would not have succeeded.

One example of these unknown women is Molly O'Reilly who, at the age of nine went to Liberty Hall to learn Irish dancing. While there she would hear James Connolly speak and was enthralled by what he had to say. During the Lockout, aged only eleven, she, with Connolly's children Roddy and Adeen would run messages from Connolly in Liberty Hall to the strikers. She helped in the soup kitchens and collected money during the Lockout. After the Howth gunrunning she hid some of the weapons in her house in Gardiner Street. All of this activity was unknown to her father who was a staunch supporter of the Crown. The week prior to the Easter Rising James Connolly specifically sent for her, via Rosie Hackett, to carry out a special request, to hoist the flag over Liberty Hall, an honour she proudly accepted. She was only fourteen years old. When the Rising began she marched to City Hall with Seán Connolly's garrison and throughout the fighting she carried messages to and from the GPO. After the Rising she went to England to train and work as a student nurse. In 1917 she returned and joined Cumann na mBan. During the War of Independence she was responsible for arranging safe houses for Volunteers who were on the run. She worked in *Bon Bouche* in Dawson Street, a coffee shop owned by Countess Markievicz and Charlotte Despard. This work enabled her to carry on her work for the nationalist movement unhindered. Her work included delivering dispatches to IRA units around the country as well as transporting arms and gelignite to the IRA in Dalkey, the unit she was assigned to. Often this work was carried out late at night and she had more than one close encounter with the Black and Tans. She took the anti-Treaty side during the Irish Civil War and was arrested in 1923. During her imprisonment she went on hunger strike and after sixteen days on the strike she was released. She later married Ned Corcoran who was a member of the 5th Battalion (Engineers) Dublin Brigade, IRA. They had five children, four boys and one girl who she named Constance after her good friend Countess Markievicz.

Another so-called ordinary woman was Brigid Davis who joined the Irish Citizen Army (ICA) in 1915. She assisted Dr Kathleen Lynn in her work preparing the women in first aid in Liberty Hall. She was a member of the City Hall garrison during the Rising, under the command of her neighbour and good friend Seán Connolly and was second in charge to Kathleen Lynn in the medical section of the ICA. She was with Seán Connolly when he was shot by a British sniper. After the surrender and arrest of the garrison she was taken to Ship Street barracks, from where she and her comrades were later transferred to Richmond Barracks and then to Kilmainham Gaol. She was released with the main body of women on 8/9 May. When the task of reorganising the ICA began she immediately returned to Liberty Hall where again she assisted Kathleen Lynn in her work. On the first anniversary of James Connolly's execution the ICA remembered their fallen leader in a way that was sure to attract the attention of the authorities. On the instigation of Helena Molony a large scroll was placed across the windows of Liberty Hall. The police were quick to take it down. Not willing to let the authorities get the better of them a new banner was quickly made. This time the women would do everything in their power to ensure the police would not remove this banner. Molony, with Rosie Hackett, Brigid Davis and Jinny Shanahan, went up to the roof of Liberty Hall. They barricaded the door to the roof and proudly unfurled their banner. These four women defied up to 400 policemen for four hours. Finally after great effort the police managed to break through the barricade and remove the banner.

In 1918 the flu epidemic was sweeping throughout the country with devastating effect. Kathleen Lynn again assisted by Brigid Davis and other ICA women did their part in helping combat the crisis. They administered vaccines to the members of the Citizen Army and their families and nursed victims of the flu in their homes.

Also in 1918 Dr Lynn with Madeleine ffrench-Mullen, Kathleen Clarke and others formed a committee with the aim of setting up a hospital for infants. Infant mortality in Dublin was amongst the highest in Europe and these women realised this problem needed to be addressed as up to that point very little was being done by the government concerning this issue. They acquired Charlemont House, which was all but a derelict building. Together with the women from the Citizen Army including Brigid Davis, they got the building in order and in 1919 St Ultan's Hospital for Sick Infants opened its doors, the first hospital of its kind in the country. Brigid Davis was again at Dr Lynn's side and in 1920 at Lynn's insistence Davis trained as a baby nurse and one year later she was fully qualified. Around this time Brigid joined Cumann na mBan. Throughout the War of Independence she carried out first aid, tending to wounded Volunteers in secret locations until they could be transferred to hospitals friendly to the IRA. That was how she met her future husband Paddy O'Duffy. A veteran of the Easter Rising he had been interned in Frongoch. Upon his release he returned to his company, 'E' Company, 2nd Battalion Dublin Brigade, IRA. During the War of Independence he was wounded, Brigid was his nurse. The two soon fell in love and married in 1921. With the signing of the Treaty and the subsequent split in the Republican movement,

O'Duffy took the pro-Treaty side. Davis took no part in the Civil War that followed. After the Civil War ended Davis settled into family life. She remained in contact with her best friend from those turbulent years, Rosie Hackett, well into old age. Brigid Davis and her husband had five children, three boys and two girls. Her eldest daughter Maureen followed in her mother's footsteps and started her career in nursing in St Ultan's hospital. Brigid Davis kept her nurse's uniform that she wore in City Hall during the Easter Rising. A uniform that she, like the other women made themselves, a uniform they were proud to wear. She put it safely away, cherishing it, unwashed, untouched, Seán Connolly's blood still visible on the shoulder where she held his head as he lay dying. Her uniform is preserved and held in Kilmainham Gaol. Brigid Davis died in 1954. She was seventy-three years old.

Finally there is Mary Hyland. Born in 1889 she, together with two of her sisters and at least four of her brothers took part in the revolutionary movement. Hyland and her brother Jim were members of the Citizen Army. She was, it seems, an early follower of the nationalist and suffrage movements. She does not appear on the 1911 Census as she refused to allow her father to put her name down until women got the vote. During the Lockout she helped in the soup kitchens in Liberty Hall. She was a singer and 'a bit of an actress' and she was regularly cast in the weekly Sunday night plays that were put on in Liberty Hall. She also helped to make the now-famous banner 'We Serve Neither King nor Kaiser but Ireland' that adorned the front of Liberty Hall. Prior to the Easter Rising she was specifically chosen by James Connolly to carry out intelligence work, which meant going to the British army barracks in the city to find out troop strength and other information that may be useful. On Easter Monday she marched with her brother Jim to St Stephen's Green under the command of Michael Mallin. Later that day she was one of a small group chosen to take over the College of Surgeons, which they held successfully until they were joined by the remaining garrison. After the surrender Hyland evaded capture. Her two brothers Jim and Thomas as well as Mick O'Kelly were arrested and sent to Frongoch. O'Kelly was also a member of the Citizen Army and had fought with Hyland in St Stephen's Green and the College of Surgeons. The two would later marry. After 1917 Hyland, it seems, took no active part in the revolutionary movement. It can be assumed that although she may not have been an active participant she no doubt gave great support to the movement considering that her brothers and husband continued their service. Her husband was imprisoned during the War of Independence and went on hunger strike. He and her brothers took the anti-Treaty side during the Civil War and again Mick was arrested. Hyland and her husband were to have five children, one boy and four girls and in later life they became the caretakers of the place that had such an effect on their lives and was most likely the place where they first met: Liberty Hall.

These three women are just some of so many forgotten or less well-known women of the Irish Revolution. But just because they are not the famous names it does not lessen or diminish their contribution to the cause of freedom but also of real social change in Ireland. The Irish Revolution was not a mass movement at first, no movement is. But through the belief and determination of many Irish men and very importantly Irish women it became a mass movement that people believed in. They did not do it for the glory or to have their names in the history books. They did it because they had the courage to stand up and give us, their future generations, a choice. The least we can do is to put their names out there and recognise just exactly what choices they gave us, whether it is in education, the freedom especially as women, to choose what career we might like to pursue, that our children have proper health care, the list goes on. This generation made a difference and for that we owe them so much.

This work forms part of *Women of the Revolution: A Photographic History* by Elizabeth Gillis (Mercier Press, 2014).

Marie Coleman

THE IRISH CITIZEN ARMY AND THE MILITARY SERVICE PENSIONS COLLECTION

THE MILITARY SERVICE PENSIONS COLLECTION

Peter Hart described Ireland's campaign for independence as one of the best documented modern revolutions in the world.[1] He wrote this in 2003 just as witness statements of the Bureau of Military History (BMH) had been released in hard copy in the National and Military Archives.[2] His observation has gained greater validity since the online release in January 2014 of phase one of the Military Service Pensions Collection (MSPC).[3] When the decision to release the MSPC was announced by the then Taoiseach Bertie Ahern in a speech at Collins Barracks on Easter Sunday 2006, to mark the ninetieth anniversary of the Rising, it was initially stated that only successful applications for military service pensions would be released; this would have amounted to documents relating to just over 18,000 individuals. In the intervening eight years there was a massive expansion of this initial remit. When the full collection is available by the centenary of the Rising in

2016 it will consist not only of the military service pensions applications, successful and unsuccessful, but also:

– applications for pensions and gratuities for those who were wounded, or dependents of those who died, during the revolution (awarded under a separate body of legislation, the Army Pensions Acts);
– pensions and gratuities awarded to former members of the Connaught Rangers regiment of the British Army who were imprisoned for their part in the mutiny in India in 1920;
– applications for service medals relating to the period 1916 to 1923;
– membership rolls for all relevant organisations (one such file for the ICA is now available)[4]

The complete collection will amount to almost 300,000 files relating to over 80,000 individuals, putting the 1,773 statements in the Bureau of Military History firmly in the shade.

THE MILITARY SERVICE PENSIONS ACTS

The first Military Service Pensions Act was passed in 1924 in response to the army mutiny of that year and restricted pension eligibility to those who had served in the named organisations (principally the Irish Volunteers, the Irish Citizen Army and Fianna Éireann) during the revolutionary years from 1916 to 1921 as well as in the Irish Army during the Civil War, leaving anti-Treaty republicans, Civil War neutrals and supporters of the Treaty who had not joined the new national army outside the benefits of the legislation.[5] In practice this proved very restrictive for members of the ICA. Twenty-four ICA members applied for pensions under the 1924 act, indicating that a small number of the force had also served in the Free State's Defence Forces during the Civil War. Conversely, some ex-ICA men, such as James O'Shea, joined the anti-Treaty IRA in 1922 and so the collection also permits of a more in-depth analysis of the treaty split upon former ICA comrades.[6]

While nationalist women were effectively disbarred from applying for pensions in 1924 because of the failure to include Cumann na mBan in the list of eligible organisations, ICA women were not nominally excluded, but by virtue of the fact that applicants had to have served in the national army they were in practice ineligible to apply. The only female member of the Irish Army between 1922 and 1980, Dr Brigid Lyons, received a pension on the grounds that she had assisted the Irish Volunteers between 1916 and 1921 even though the organisation of which she was a member was Cumann na mBan.[7] Therefore, the vast majority of ICA members who were awarded military service pensions, including all of the women, received them under the terms of the 1934 Military Service Pensions Act, which extended eligibility to republicans, Civil War neutrals and Cumann na mBan. The majority of all military service pensions were awarded at the lower levels (E and D under the 1934 act, and A and B under the 1924 act). Very few in the ICA received pensions commensurate to higher ranks. Margaret Skinnider, who was initially refused a disability pension under the 1923 Army Pensions Act on the grounds that the legislation was 'only applicable to soldiers as generally understood in the masculine sense',[8] eventually received her wound pension when the legislation was amended in 1927 to replace the terms 'officer or soldier' with 'person'.[9] She also received the highest grade ('D') of any of the ICA women who were awarded military service pensions. The highest ranking ICA pensioner (at Grade 'C' under the 1934 act) was James O'Neill, who was active in the ICA throughout the period from the Rising until the end of the War of Independence.[10]

THE MILITARY SERVICE PENSIONS COLLECTION AND THE IRISH CITIZEN ARMY

The value of the MSPC is especially noticeable with regard to the smaller organisations like Cumann na mBan, Fianna

Éireann and the Irish Citizen Army. The Bureau of Military History contains approximately nineteen statements from members of the ICA or people who were associated with it. This has enabled historians to give a much greater insight into the contribution of the ICA to the Rising, as seen in the recent studies of the rebellion by Charles Townshend and Fearghal McGarry.[11] By contrast the first phase of the MSPC contains files relating to 219 individuals who were either members or associates of the ICA. It can be difficult to gauge the exact number of ICA members covered by these collections as some were members of more than one organisation; for example, Helena Molony's BMH statement lists her as a primarily member of Inghinidhe na hÉireann and Cumann na mBan, whereas her application for a military service pension was based on her association with the ICA. This level of cross-fertilisation between the ICA and the nationalist organisations, the Irish Volunteers and Cumann na mBan, is one aspect of the experience of the ICA on which the MSPC throws greater light.

The BMH allowed historians to provide a more nuanced picture of the role of women within the ICA, thanks to the statements from six leading female members: Nellie Gifford (Donnelly), Helena Molony, Dr Kathleen Lynn, Maeve Cavanagh (McDowell), Marie Perolz and the subject of this book, Rosie Hackett. Five of these (Kathleen Lynn excepted) applied for and were awarded military service pensions, so we now have additional archival testimony from them. However, as the MSPC is much broader in scope, there are documents relating to twenty-one additional ICA women members and associates now available which will allow for an even more in-depth analysis of the role of women in the ICA. The MSPC gives a much greater insight into family connections within the ICA. Of particular interest in this regard are the applications of the three Poole brothers, Christopher,

Vincent and Patrick, and Patrick's son, John. Unlike the Pooles, all of whom served in the ICA, some brothers served across different organisations, such as Frederick and Francis Henry of the ICA, whose brother James was in the Irish Volunteers; the application of a fourth brother, Robert, has yet to be released. Sisters who were in the ICA, and whose service is outlined in more detail in the collection include the Connollys; Ina Connolly-Heron and Nora Connolly-O'Brien, while the Giffords are a good example of membership across different organisations, Nellie (Donnelly) in the ICA and Sidney Czira in Cumann na mBan. Their two sisters who were widowed as a result of the Rising (Grace Plunkett and Muriel MacDonagh) also feature in the collection.

There was also a significant level of inter-generational membership of the ICA within families. The most obvious example of this was James and Roddy Connolly, but also Frederick and Alfred Norgrove and Richard and Laurence Corbally. This contrasts with the Irish Volunteers where it was very unusual to find fathers and sons in that organisation, which tended to be composed primarily of the younger men. If the older generation was involved in a nationalist organisation it was more likely to have been in Sinn Féin. Some of the women whose files are now available were the female relatives of well-known ICA members; for example the MSPC contains the unsuccessful pension application of Christina Crothers (Hunter), sister of Christopher Crothers, whereas the BMH has only her brother's statement. Another sibling who applied unsuccessfully was Kathleen Mallin (Rossiter), a sister of Michael Mallin, one of the highest profile members of the ICA to be executed after the Rising. Mallin's brothers, Bartle and John, served in the Volunteers and Bartle was awarded a pension but John was not. The executions meant that the personal voices of many of the key participants would not appear in the subsequent archival memory. Therefore, the inclusion of applications for allowances and pensions for dependents, made under the Army Pensions Acts, means that we have captured the voices of their closest family and have a unique new insight into the personal, social and financial circumstances of the families of men who died as a result of the fighting or were subsequently executed. Phase one of the MSPC contains details of allowances paid to the widows of eleven ICA men who died as a result of the Rising, including James Connolly, Michael Mallin and Sean Connolly, in addition to allowances paid to dependents of five more ICA fatalities. The impact of the Rising on these families comes across in applications such as that of Margaret Geoghegan, widow of the ICA's George Geoghegan, who in 1924 was 'in poor circumstances ... living in the top back room of [a] tenement house' in Upper Dorset Street, along with her three children. The meagre allowances which the White Cross had been able to provide had dried up and her only income was from casual work as a charwoman. The award of an annual allowance of £162 (£90 for herself and £24 for each of her children) must have improved the family's circumstances considerably.[12]

ROSIE HACKETT'S MILITARY SERVICE PENSION

One legitimate criticism of the BMH as a source relates to its reliability given that the interviews were held in the 1950s, 30 or 40 years after the events which were described had taken place, and errors of memory and fact continue to be found in many statements. However, the release of the MSPC raises the question of the extent to which the BMH was a reflection of veterans' memories from the 1950s. In the case of those who gave BMH statements and were awarded pensions it is possible that their pension applications formed the basis of the subsequent witness statements. This is noticeable when comparing both documents in regard to Rosie Hackett. Her BMH statement related essentially to her role in the ICA between 1913 and 1917 and describes her work in preparing for the Rising, including defending Liberty Hall from a police raid in search of the St Patrick's Day issue of *The Gael* in March 1916; her mobilisation at Liberty Hall and subsequent first aid work while attached to the College of Surgeons garrison in Easter Week; her arrest and short-term imprisonment for ten days after the Rising; and her role in barricading Liberty Hall during the Connolly commemoration on the first anniversary of James Connolly's death in May 1917.[13]

Her pension application throws more light on her work after the Rising; she left the ICA in 1918 and was briefly a member of Cumann na mBan in Fairview during 1919 and 1920. She does not appear to have been very active during these latter years and did not seek any pension based on her service at this time. Her Certificate of Military Service, and her subsequent pension, awarded her the equivalent of four years of pension service for her activities during Easter Week (this was the full amount of service that could be given for Easter Week service under the 1934 act) and 8/179 of one year for her subsequent work in the year to the end of March 1917. This entitled her to a pension of £20–4–6 in 1936 (which had risen to £122.88 by 1974).[14] While her witness statement, given in May 1951, is the longer and more detailed document, the content is largely similar to her application for a military service pension made fifteen years prior to this in 1936. Therefore, there is a need to reassess the view of the BMH as representing the memory of its interviewees up to forty years after the events they described. These witness statements are clearly the much later memory of the interviewees, but it is possible that this memory is closer to the revolutionary period that has previously been credited.

Rosie Hackett's pension application is also illustrative of the personal circumstances of the applicants and their dependents that is revealed by the documents in the MSPC. In many cases these reveal the poor circumstances – socially, financially and in regard to health – that veterans of the independence campaign and their families subsequently found themselves in. In Rosie Hackett's case her file makes for sombre reading where the final stages of her mental and physical well-being are concerned. In 1973 her half-brother Thomas Gray, wrote to the Department of Defence stating that 'My sister Rosanna Hackett, who is over 80 years of age is at present in St Vincent's Hospital, Convent Avenue, Richmond Road, Fairview, Dublin, and is unable to complete this form owing to mental illness'.[15] The exact details of her illness were not outlined but it is possible that her advanced age was a factor, and she was made a ward of court in 1974 until her death in 1976.

CONCLUSION

As the centenary of the Easter Rising approaches we are now getting a much fuller picture of the militia that is sometimes seen as the poor relation of the Irish Volunteers. The Irish Citizen Army was in many ways a family affair, composed of siblings – both brothers and sisters – but also of parents and their youth or young adult children. Membership of the ICA was not exclusive, with some male members also serving in the Volunteers and females in Cumann na mBan at various times during the revolutionary years. The treaty split also divided ex-ICA comrades. Perhaps most importantly, the files relating to the award of wound pensions to those who were injured and to the dependents of those who perished in Easter Week, provide an insight that has been lacking to date in the archival sources, that details the human cost of the campaign for Irish independence.

NOTES

1   Peter Hart, 'A new revolutionary history' in *The IRA at War, 1916–1923* (Oxford, 2003), p. 5.

2   Now available online www.bureauofmilitaryhistory.ie

3   http://www.militaryarchives.ie/collections/online-collections/military-service-pensions-collection.

4   MA/MSPC/RO10A.

5   For more details on the legislation and the background to its introduction, see Marie Coleman, 'Military Service Pensions for veterans of the Irish revolution, 1916–1923', *War in History*, 20: 2 (April 2013), pp 201–21.

6   MA/MSPA/W34E207: James O'Shea.

7   MA/MSPC/W24C1295: Brigid Lyons; MA/MSPC/SP13615: Brigid Lyons.

8   Treasury Solicitor to Army Finance Officer, 18 March 1925, MA/MSPC/W1P724: Margaret Skinnider.

9   Army Pensions Act, 1927, First Schedule.

10 MA/MSPC/MSP34REF8368.

11 Charles Townshend, *Easter 1916: The Irish Rebellion* (Penguin, 2005); Fearghal McGarry, *The Rising: Ireland, Easter 1916* (Oxford, 2010).

12 MA/MSPC/WC19: George Geoghegan; MA/MSPC/W1D43: George Geoghegan.

13 BMH WS546: Rosie Hackett.

14 MA/MSPC/WMSP34REF20787: Rosanna Hackett; MA/MSPC/W34E2128: Rosanna Hackett.

15 MA/MSPC/W34E2128: Rosanna Hackett.

Fearghal McGarry

HELENA MOLONY:
REBEL AND ACTIVIST

It was as a result of the big strike in 1913 that I first became
attached to Liberty Hall. A workroom was opened to assist
girls who had lost their employment as a result of the strike ...
Miss Helena Molony came to take charge, and that is when the
work of the women's section of the Irish Citizen Army started
in earnest

– Rosie Hackett[1]

Dublin City Council's decision to name the new bridge
over the Liffey after Rosie Hackett can be seen as a
welcome, if long overdue, acknowledgement of the role of
women in the struggle for social and political liberation.
The timing was appropriate, coinciding as it did with the
centenary of the Lockout, and a wider debate about the
nature of the Irish Republic prompted by the current
economic crisis.[2] While the achievements of radical women
such as Rosie Hackett deserve to be remembered, it is also
important to consider why such figures were for so long
written out of history.[3] This essay explores how the radical
vision of Helena Molony, another trade-unionist and rebel,

came to be marginalised following the Easter Rising which she, and Hackett, had helped to bring about. Born in Dublin in 1883, Helena Molony was, like many of her revolutionary generation radicalised by the cultural revival and the wave of activism triggered by the 1798 centenary, the royal visits of 1900 and 1903, and anti-Boer War agitation. She joined Inghinidhe na hÉireann, established in 1900 by Maud Gonne to advocate feminism, separatism and militancy.[4] Editor of *Bean na hÉireann,* and a founding member of Na Fianna Éireann (founded by her friend Countess Markievicz), Molony was a prominent separatist, becoming the first female political prisoner of her generation when she was arrested during George V's 1911 visit. She was, by then, attracted to James Connolly's revolutionary socialism, 'I was fumbling at the idea of a junction between labour and nationalism', she explained, 'Labour and the Nation were really one'. Like many radical women, she also admired his egalitarianism, 'Connolly, staunch feminist that he was, was more than anxious to welcome women into the ranks on equal terms with men'. Her embrace of socialism was reinforced by her involvement in the Lockout when she worked in Liberty Hall's food kitchen and addressed strike meetings. An Abbey actor, she drew on her theatrical experience to disguise Jim Larkin (whom she disliked) as an elderly clergyman to facilitate his famous appearance on the balcony of the Imperial Hotel during the 1913 Lockout. The Lockout, Molony believed, 'profoundly affected the whole country', producing 'a sort of social and intellectual revolution'. It also contributed to a personal breakdown, leading her to spend much of 1914 convalescing in France with Maud Gonne.

On her return Molony drew closer to Connolly, she ran the workers' co-operative store adjoining Liberty Hall (where Rosie Hackett worked), succeeded Delia Larkin as general secretary of the beleaguered Irish Women

Workers' Union (IWWU), and became proprietor of Connolly's *Workers' Republic*. She also drilled 'the girls as a unit of the [Irish] Citizen Army', a force she regarded as more militant than the Irish Volunteers and the Irish Republican Brotherhood due to its unequivocal commitment to the necessity for revolutionary violence. She was also critical of Cumann na mBan's subordinate role, emphasising, more than was justified, the Citizen Army's egalitarianism, 'even before the Russian army had women soldiers, the Citizen Army had them'. Molony's willingness to use violence for political ends was not in doubt, as Rosie Hackett's description of a police raid on Liberty Hall demonstrates:

> The policeman was behind the counter. Connolly rushed down as quickly as he could. He just saw them with the papers and said: 'Drop them, or I will drop you'. Helena must have come in, as she was standing at the fireplace with her weapon ready, in case Connolly was attacked. She always had a gun, and was always prepared. When Connolly said: 'Drop them, or I will drop you', he had them covered from that on. The police went off, and came back later with a warrant. They searched around, but they got nothing. I had hidden the stuff.[5]

Liberty Hall remained under armed guard in the days that followed, 'the atmosphere', Molony recalled, 'was like a simmering pot'. Unwilling to miss the rebellion, she spent the fortnight before Easter 'sleeping at night on a pile of men's coats in the back of the shop'. Both she and Hackett were involved in the Military Council's secret preparations for the rebellion. Rosie assisted in the printing of the Proclamation, copies of which were hidden under Molony's pillow on the night before the Rising.[6] Like many rebels, Molony recalled the insurrection in euphoric terms, 'When we walked out that Easter Monday morning we felt in a very real sense that we were walking with Ireland into the sun'. She participated in the Citizen Army's dramatic raid on Dublin Castle, which resulted in the death of an unarmed policeman, but her rebellion proved short-lived.

Captured when City Hall fell, she spent the week imprisoned in a filthy room in Ship Street barracks. After the Rising she was transferred to Kilmainham where she was shaken by the executions – 'Connolly was dragged out, unable to stand, and murdered. After that life seemed to come to an end for me'. Following a spirited, if unsuccessful, attempt to burrow out of Kilmainham Jail with a spoon, she became one of only five women among over 2,500 internees sent to England. There she continued to cause problems for the authorities, using her links with Sylvia Pankhurst's Workers' Suffrage Federation to publicise conditions in the grim Victorian jail at Aylesbury, where she was interred.

Throughout her life, Molony regarded the Rising as the high point in the struggle for liberty. Returning to Liberty Hall in 1917, she described how Connolly's execution had resulted in a shift from insurrectionary republicanism, 'The Union was in the hands of Larkin's section. The Hall was in their hands too. We knew we had unsympathetic members in the back, and enemies in the front'. Molony and Hackett nonetheless ensured that the anniversary of Connolly's execution was commemorated at Liberty Hall, defiantly barricading themselves onto the roof to unfurl a banner: 'James Connolly Murdered May 12th, 1916'. Despite Molony's efforts, women were marginalised within the republican movement that emerged from the ashes of the Rising. Although she was hastily added to the Mansion House Committee after denouncing its exclusion of women in April 1917, women were excluded from the leadership following the subsequent merger between Sinn Féin and the Liberty Clubs. Despite pointing out 'the risk women took, equally with the men, to have the Republic established', the League of Women Delegates' demands for representation on Sinn Féin's executive were ignored.[7] Although Molony and three other women were eventually co-opted, only twelve women attended the thousand-strong Sinn Féin convention, while only two contested the 1918 general election. There was to be little political space for women within this new Ireland.

Molony played a minor role in the revolution that followed. During the War of Independence she was a district justice at Rathmines, and enrolled as a member of Cumann na mBan (although she refused to wear the uniform). She participated in the usual range of women's roles: first-aid, procuring and concealing weapons, prisoner welfare, intelligence and publicity work.[8] Her activities rendered her a frequent target of arrests and raids by the British, and during the Civil War when she opposed the Treaty, by the Free State authorities.

After the revolution, Molony, like Hackett, devoted herself to the Irish Women Workers' Union. Although replaced as general secretary by Louie Bennett in 1918, she was its organising secretary between 1929 and 1941, a period that saw modest expansion in a difficult economic and political environment. She campaigned against the undermining of the principle of equality enshrined in the Proclamation, noting bitterly how, despite winning the vote, Irish women retained:

> their inferior status, their lower pay for equal work, their exclusion from juries and certain branches of the civil service, their slum dwellings and crowded, cold and unsanitary schools for their children.[9]

Her campaigns won little support from the Labour Party, whose treatyite politics she condemned, or the male-dominated trade-union movement. 'Woman is the queen of our hearts and of our homes', declared one T.U.C. delegate confronted by Molony's motion against the discriminatory Conditions of Employment Bill, 'and, for God's sake, let us try to keep her there'.[10]

Molony's public criticism of the Vatican, support for the IRA, and defence of the Soviet Union (which she visited) reinforced her marginalisation, including within her own trade union where her republican and socialist militancy created tensions. Although elected president of the Irish Trade Union Congress in 1937, only the second woman to hold the office, she was forced to retire from the IWWU in 1941. Although attributed to her poor health, alcoholism, depression and her links to the wartime IRA played a role in ending her career in public life. She lived in straitened circumstances, dependent on appeals to friends and her former trade union. Her relationship with psychiatrist Evelyn O'Brien, with whom she lived until her death in 1967, has led some to claim Molony as a member of an influential network of lesbians prominent in overlapping feminist, socialist, trade union and republican circles whose sexuality remained largely hidden from history,[11] however she was also linked romantically to Bulmer Hobson, and to Seán Connolly who died in her arms on the roof of City Hall. Well-founded or not, such speculation highlights the relationship between gender, sexuality and power in post-revolutionary Ireland and the troubling status of unmarried or independent-minded women in a society which valued women as mothers rather than citizens.

Revolutions, like political lives, tend to end in disappointment. Irish republicanism triumphed after 1916 but the state that emerged from Sinn Féin's revolution fell short of the radical vision for which Molony had struggled, a vision that encompassed social and economic, as well as, political emancipation. The failure to transform society was partly a result of the polarisation brought about by revolutionary violence and partition, but it also reflected the ideological incoherence of republicanism, and the limited appeal of the radicalism that inspired a tiny minority before 1916. 'Perhaps the time was not ripe for success', Molony conceded, 'I should have hated to see Padraic Pearse as President of an Irish Republic if the misery and wretchedness of the tenements had still gone on'.[12]

Molony's experiences highlight how the abstraction that was the Irish nation was shaped by the harsh realities of class, gender and power. The contribution of radicals like Molony was elided as the Irish state constructed a narrative of its liberation reflecting the Catholic nationalist ethos that held sway after 1916. Conscious of the marginalisation of women's role in the struggle for independence, Molony entered into a lengthy dispute with the Military Pensions advisory committee over its refusal to classify much of her work during the revolution as military service. She was 'not primarily concerned with a pension', she asserted, 'but with the recognition of women's services rendered to the Republic'.[13] Despite the poignant gulf between aspiration and outcome, Molony remained proud of her role in the rebellion. Writing in 1935, when the myth of the Rising as a Christ-like blood sacrifice had been firmly established, she continued to articulate an alternative narrative of struggle, one that retains contemporary relevance given the inequality of present-day society:

> 1916 has been represented as a gesture of sacrifice. It is said that those in it knew they would be defeated ... I know how we all felt. We thought we were going to do this big thing, to free our country. It was like a religion – something that filled the whole of life. Personal feelings and vanities, wealth, comfort, position – these things did not matter ... Everyone was exalted and caught in the sweep of a great movement. We saw a vision of Ireland, free, pure, happy. We did not realise this vision. But we saw it.[14]

NOTES

1   BMH WS 546 (Rose Hackett), Military Archives.
2   Fintan O'Toole, *Enough is enough: how to build a new republic* (London, 2010).

3   Two important biographical accounts are Nell Regan's 'Helena Molony', in Mary Cullen and Maria Luddy (eds), *Female activists. Irish women and change 1900–1960* (Dublin, 2000) and Penny Duggan's *Helena Molony: actress, feminist, nationalist, socialist and trade-unionist* (Amsterdam, 1990).

4   BMH WS 391 (Helena Molony). Subsequent quotes are derived from this source unless specified.

5   BMH WS 546 (Rose Hackett).

6   BMH WS 705 (Christopher Brady).

7   Margaret Ward, 'The League of Women Delegates and Sinn Féin', *History Ireland*, 4/3 (Autumn, 1996), pp 37–41.

8   'Sworn statement by Helena Moloney', 3 July 1936, Military Pension file 11739, Military Archives.

9   Helena Molony, 'James Connolly and women', *Dublin Labour Year Book* (1930).

10 Mary Jones, *These obstreperous lassies: a history of the IWWU* (Dublin, 1988), p. 129.

11 Marie Mullholland, *The politics and relationships of Kathleen Lynn* (Dublin, 2002), pp 6–19.

12 R. M. Fox, *Rebel Irishwomen* (Dublin, 1935), p. 127.

13 Molony to Advisory Committee, 18 November 1936, Military Pension file 11739.

14 Fox, *Rebel Irishwomen*, pp 131–2.

Rosemary Cullen Owens

LOUIE BENNETT AND THE
IRISH WOMEN WORKERS' UNION

The formation of the Irish Women Workers' Union
(IWWU) in 1911 was a particularly significant
development, both for the role it would play in improving
pay and working conditions for women and for the high
profile attained by its women leaders. Its foundation
followed a successful strike for better pay by 3000 women
at Jacob's biscuit factory in Dublin in 1911. Delia Larkin
was its first Secretary, and Jim Larkin its President. During
the subsequent Dublin Lockout of 1913, the entire
membership of the IWWU came out on strike in support,
remaining out for six months. Many were dismissed
subsequently for their action. In 1915, Helena Molony took
over Delia Larkin's role in the IWWU, following the
latter's departure for Liverpool. Shortly before the 1916
Rising, Molony sought the help of suffragist Louie Bennett
in re-organising the IWWU. Following Molony's request,
Bennett had a 'warm discussion' with James Connolly
during which she argued against his mixing of nationalist

and labour ideals. Although anxious to help, Bennett made it clear that as a pacifist she could not support any organisation threatening force. Imprisoned after the Rising of 1916, Molony made a further appeal to Bennett for help with the IWWU. This time Bennett responded positively, and in August 1916 she and Helen Chenevix attended the Trade Union Congress in Sligo. From that time she became identified with the work of the IWWU, an association which would continue for the next forty years. Gains achieved by the IWWU over the coming decades in many ways were disproportionate to its membership and were to a large extent the result of the commitment of these women to the rights of women workers and women generally.

Bennett viewed her attendance at that 1916 Congress as a first step in her trade union education. Through the pages of the *Irish Citizen* she expressed views similar to those of Connolly:

> The rapid development of organisation in the Irishwomen's world of labour is the best possible contribution to the whole cause of feminism. There can be no real freedom and independence of women until they are economically free.[1]

So began what she described as a 'timid campaign' of waiting outside printers' workshops at six o'clock in the evening thrusting handbills upon disinterested women workers. Initially there was little reaction, but eventually:

> there came a stir and a rush: Mondays evenings saw the long room packed with girls and women eager to pay their pennies and to pour their grievances into my confused ear.[2]

Soon women from other industries came to join, and a bigger office was opened in Dame Street. Within months, membership was over 2000 and growing, and included women in the printing, box-making, laundry and textile industries. In the spring of 1918 the IWWU was officially registered as a trade union with Bennett and Chenevix as its honorary secretaries. By this time membership exceeded 5,000.

From the outset Bennett insisted that the women's union operate independently from Liberty Hall and remain solely a women's union, a point of much debate over the years. In negotiations with employers, Bennett's policy would be conciliatory rather than confrontational. From the beginning union policy concentrated as much on improving working conditions as on wage increases. Bennett maintained that whereas wages were the primary concern of male workers, for women workers conditions were equally important, declaring 'Holidays, shorter hours, and a little latitude as to spells of leisure during working hours, are concessions dear to women in factories or workshops'.[3] Bennett's close identification with Labour did not inhibit criticism where she felt it necessary. During the Irish Convention of 1917, the *Irish Citizen* reported:

> When Labour Sunday was celebrated in Dublin a few weeks ago, no woman was invited to stand on the platform by the Labour Party. The women of Ireland might have all been free to enjoy the comforts of a home, a fireside, and a cradle to rock for all the interest the Labour Party of Ireland manifested in their affairs.[4]

In the post-war and (limited) post-suffrage situation, was the continuation of women in a separate union still the best method of organization for women workers or was the 'one big union' a better idea? Late in 1919, a lively debate took place on this issue between Bennett and Cissie Cahalan of the Drapers Assistant Association (DAA) in the pages of the *Irish Citizen*. Advocating separate organization, Bennett argued:

> There is a disposition amongst men workers not only to keep women in inferior and subordinate positions, but to drive them out of industry altogether. Moreover, men have not the same aspirations for women as women have for themselves, and in a mixed organisation much time and trouble would

> have to be wasted in securing the co-operation of men in a demand for reforms of which women may feel urgent need.[5]

In addition she noted that pay increases demanded and accepted for women workers within mixed unions were almost always considerably less than those obtained for men. Cissie Cahalan, one of the few examples of working-class involvement in the Irish suffrage movement, defended the concept of mixed trade unions. She argued that women's reluctance to go forward as candidates for branch or executive committees left the management of trade unions in male hands. Women's position in the labour movement she said while weak was not subordinate, and could become stronger if women ceased to be apathetic and took up their responsibilities. She claimed that if women in the industrial world want a place in the labour movement, they must seek it in the Labour Parliament, shoulder to shoulder with the men and not in any separate organisation apart and isolated. The arguments raised in this debate continued for many years, Bennett's involvement within the trade union movement reinforcing her beliefs. In 1930 she noted that but for the IWWU, woman's voice was rarely heard at trades union congress or trades council, pointing to large areas of women's employment – teachers, clerical workers, shop assistants – which were almost always represented by men. Interestingly her critic from 1919, Cissie Cahalan, writing in the same journal observed that it was 'deplorable to find men who still think of woman as the enemy – and shut their eyes to the real barrier to a full and complete life for all – the capitalist class'.[6]

While disagreement with Bennett's views concentrated mainly on the issue of single-sex unions, little criticism was voiced towards her views regarding women's right to work. Bennett did not believe the time was right for women to 'invade' men's industrial preserves, claiming that 'the class war must be fought out before women could fight for equality of opportunity'.[7] Bennett's views were reinforced over the following years when deteriorating employment opportunities in Ireland became allied to an increased perception of the woman worker as a threat. Trade union and labour acceptance of church, state and societal convergence on the ideal of a family wage, removing the need for married women to work outside the home, would be reinforced by legislative restrictions during the 1930s.

While Bennett's preference for negotiation rather than confrontation was well known, when necessary strikes there were and none more noteworthy than the Laundry workers strike. In 1945 laundry worker members of the IWWU voted for strike action to obtain a fortnight's paid holiday. Laundresses had sought increased holidays, reduction in overtime and regular working hours from 1934. Their claims had been shelved during the war years, employers refusing to negotiate. An exception to this was the Court Laundry which, in 1944, unofficially agreed to a second week's paid holiday. As a result the Court was the only laundry to function during the strike. Now the claim for two week's holiday became a political issue. Working conditions in laundries were particularly bad. The IWWU placed much emphasis on the health risks involved in laundry work, arguing that shorter hours and extra holidays were necessary to minimise such risks. In rejecting IWWU demand, the Federated Union of Employers (FUE) intimated that no increased holidays would be granted until the government declared a statutory fortnight's paid holiday. Despite discussions between the ITUC and the FUE, no resolution was reached. On 21 July 1945, 1,500 women commenced strike action that would last fourteen weeks.

Bennett laid the blame for the strike directly on the shoulders of the employers. Writing to the press she made it quite clear that the FUE, and not the IWWU, were responsible for the deadlock. Before the advent of the home washing machine, laundry customers were both domestic and commercial. Despite the great inconvenience caused it soon became clear that the striking women had public opinion on their side. Despite the fact that at this time the trade union movement was torn by dissent, and had in fact split into rival congresses, support for the strikers came from all sides. The strikers themselves kept morale going with regular meetings, parades, media coverage, and the sale of a strike song, sung to the air of the war-time song 'Lily Marlene', sold at 1d a sheet. Mai Clifford, a participant in the strike, later recounted that 'efforts to dampen such enthusiasm were pressed by the employers through various media campaigns waged against the general secretary, Louie Bennett'.[8] Ultimately the women were successful in their claim, and as in the case of official tea-breaks introduced some years earlier, set an example quickly followed by male workers. Clifford noted that the successful outcome to the strike 'gave an enormous boost to the union and heightened the profile of the IWWU as a militant and progressive union'.[9]

Despite the Conditions of Employment Act, 1936, which sought to restrict women's participation in the workforce, the number of women employed in new industries grew steadily during the 1930s, although this had not been the objective of either government or most trade unions. This fact was not ignored for too long by mainstream unions, and from this point on most growth in female trade union membership took place in mixed unions and in clerical and white-collar unions.

Despite a continuing fall in numbers, the IWWU remained in existence until 1984 when it amalgamated with the Federated Workers' Union of Ireland (FWUL). A number of factors contributed to its decline, the virtual disappearance of commercial laundries, increasing mechanisation, and increasingly, women's membership of mixed unions. Without doubt, the IWWU had played a leading role in advancing the cause of women, not solely within the workplace, but also within the labour movement. At its peak of activity from the 1920s–1940s, the union operated against a backdrop of economic hardship, emigration and war. In addition it had to fight not just employers, but perhaps more significantly, other groups within the trade union and Labour movement who resisted an expansion of women's role. Its leaders were the only trade unionists consistently articulating the concerns of women workers. In retrospect, it can be seen as both the victor and victim during the years of its existence. Reflecting on the achievements of women workers to a teachers' group in 1947, Bennett recounted the horrific conditions of women workers in 1917, underpaid and exploited, working a fifty-four hour week, sixty in laundries, with no paid holidays. She credited women for the considerable reforms achieved in working conditions over the previous 30 years, pointing out that:

> It was the women workers who inflamed the campaign which won shorter working hours, the extension of the annual holiday, the break in the five-hour shift. And it is the women workers who are leading the drive for amended factory laws, a higher standard of health services and of hygienic environment. Women's influence has in fact proved a humanising factor in industry.[10]

Following Bennett's breaking of the gender stereotype by becoming the first woman president of the International Trade Union Confederation (ITUC) in 1932, her colleagues Helen Chenevix and Helena Molony followed in her footsteps. In her late seventies she served a second term as ITUC president 1947–48. While she dallied with the idea of retirement from her position as General Secretary of the IWWU from 1950, it was not until early 1955 that she actually retired. She died at her home on 25 November 1956. She was almost 87 years of age. Described by Ruaidhri Roberts as 'one of the most significant trade union leaders of the period', John Swift remembered her as 'one for whom democracy was measured, not by the privileges claimed by the majority, but by the rights assured to the minority'.[11]

NOTES

1   Rosemary Owens 'Votes for Ladies, Votes for Women'; Organised Labour and the Suffrage Movement, 1876–1922 in *Saothar* 9 (1983), pp 35–6.

2   Louie Bennett 'With the Irish Women Workers;' in *Irish Economist*, vols 7–8 (August 1922), pp 294–301.

3   Bennett 'With the Irish Women Workers' p. 298.

4   *Irish Citizen*, July 1917.

5   *Irish Citizen*, November 1919.

6   Rosemary Cullen Owens *A Social History of Women in Ireland, 1870–1970* (Dublin; 2005), p. 202.

7   *Ibid.*

8   *Ibid*, p. 212.

9   *Ibid.*

10   *Ibid.*

11   Rosemary Cullen Owens *Louie Bennett* (Cork; 2001), pp 130–132.

Therese Caherty

HISTORY IS WRITTEN BY THE VICTORS

We've all heard that said and we know that traditionally, power puts ink in the pens of those who record events for posterity. The people of the 1913 Lockout did not get the chance to have their side of the story fairly told, and this was just one of the many obstacles the strikers and their families faced. For all the disappointments and defeats of the last few years here in Ireland, as least we have a trade union movement capable of ensuring that their story is heard now.

One such story is that of 16-year-old Alicia Brady, who was described at her funeral by James Connolly as 'as true a martyr for Irish freedom as any whoever died in Ireland'. She was one of the earliest members of the Irish Women Workers' Union (IWWU). As is so often the case with those times, the details of her life are sketchy. It was suggested at her graveside a century ago that she might have grown up to be an outstanding contributor to the labour movement in particular and society in general. Would that have been the case? None of us can answer that question.

Given Alicia's circumstances, it seems more likely that had she survived she would have returned to her job when the Lockout ended, continued to work long and hard for terribly little money until she married and had her own family. At that point her fortunes would have depended on who she knew, where she lived and whether, perhaps, she could continue to work. This, of course, was a 'privilege' enjoyed by few married women of her day. Jacob's, for instance, a firm whose name is inextricably linked with the Lockout, was generally considered a good employer around that time but it did not, as a matter of policy, employ married women. Those who were there long enough were given a wedding cake as a parting gift when they left to wed and the only circumstances in which they might return to the company's workforce was if they were widowed. Inequalities in the workplace, of course, persist to this day and the role of the IWWU in battling through a large part of the 20th century is one of the reasons we celebrate its work today. For Alicia, as much as anything her fate would have depended on whether she had chosen her husband well and whether he, in turn, was lucky in his work and conscientious about his family. Her life, in effect, like the lives of so many women who lived at that time, would have consisted of lotteries within lotteries in which she would have had little say over the picking of the numbers. Indeed, if she had lived, we might never have heard of Alicia Brady. She would have been like the many thousands of other women who have passed quietly into history without their names ever meriting a mention in its books.

As it is, she became an unwitting martyr. Although that was undoubtedly the furthest thing from her mind the day she got caught up in the challenge to strike breakers near St Mark's Church on Pearse Street. But how could that diminish the scale of her sacrifice? Alicia's death reminds us that the women who were part of the struggle in 1913 did not just run the soup kitchens, run the households or tend the wounds of the men returning from the picket lines. They did all of that and they were also on the frontline. In 1911, the year the IWWU was founded in the Antient Concert Rooms on Dublin's Brunswick St, now Pearse Street, British suffragette Christabel Pankhurst said, 'We are here to claim our right as women, not only to be free, but to fight for freedom. That is our right as well as our duty'. Alicia Brady asserted that right; she fulfilled that duty and paid a heavy price. The IWWU Commemorative Committee works to remember her name, acknowledge her bravery and in so doing remember all those whose names have slipped, unacknowledged into time.

Happily, one who has not slipped away unacknowledged is Rosie Hackett whose own life and contribution to the events of a century ago have recently been recognised by the members of Dublin City Council. They voted in 2013 to name the new bridge linking Eden Quay and Burgh Quay after her. Their decision was based not just on Rosie's remarkable life and achievements but also on what she represented, a woman often having to fight for the right to fight in a world utterly dominated by men, whether rich or poor. During the campaign to persuade Dublin City councillors to bestow that honour on Rosie we encountered great difficulty in verifying the details of her life. That difficulty really hammered home the extent to which the contributions of so many women have been downplayed, underappreciated or simply ignored through the years. It also highlighted the crying need for more solid research into the roles they played throughout our history.

The IWWU showed what could be achieved by women working together sometimes, though not always, with the support of the wider trade union movement. But even the IWWU's successes took a long time to receive the recognition they deserved because half a century after the Lockout, the workers might have acquired a few rights but women were still struggling to win control of the typewriters. Essentially, the IWWU Commemorative Committee was formed to help to ensure that the story of the union and its members, such as Alicia Brady and Rosie Hackett, are told. In that quest, the support we got from the modern day trade union movement suggests that change is afoot. Still, at the end of a year in which the country struggled miserably to grapple with the implications of what happened to Savita Halappanavar and most of us did little after over a thousand workers, almost all women, were killed in a factory collapse in Bangladesh, apart from shrugging our shoulders and continuing to queue for cheap clothes in Penneys, Mango, C&A, it's clear that the struggle is not over.

Alicia lived and died at a time when the reverberations of the Triangle Shirtwaist Factory disaster in New York were being felt in the labour movement internationally. The fire that broke out on the afternoon of 25 March 1911 was considered one of the worst factory accidents in the city's history. Almost 150 people died, 123 of them women. Locked doors (to prevent break-ins and stealing) meant many jumped from the flames to their deaths from the eighth, ninth and tenth floors where the company was based while others burned to death. The Triangle normally employed about 500 workers, mostly young immigrant women, who worked nine hours a day on weekdays plus seven hours on Saturdays, earning between $7 and $12 a week. Young Alicia Brady would have easily related to the struggles of those garment workers in Savar, Dhaka, forced to work in a dangerous building, earning little more than €38 a month, being treated as little better than slaves. One of the deadliest garment-factory accidents in history, the modern-day dire working conditions are almost a replay of those that led to that Triangle Factory fire over a century before. Alicia Brady and Rosie Hackett would, I am sure, want us to see the fight of those Bangladeshi women and girls as a continuation of theirs. But then the struggle for women's rights is inextricably linked to the fight for trade union rights and, important as it is to recall the life and death of Alicia Brady and the struggles of Rosie Hackett, it would be so much better, more substantial and so much more an enduring and meaningful tribute if we embrace their cause as our own and resolve to fight until victory is achieved, no matter how long that takes. It won't be easy. It never is. But we have to try; we owe that much to all the women of 1913. We owe it to the millions of women all over the world who do not have the wherewithal to fight the fight for themselves and we owe it, for the sacrifice made one hundred years ago by young working women like Alicia Brady and by others who fought long and hard for working women's rights, like her contemporary, Rosie Hackett.

Lauren Arrington is Senior Lecturer at the Institute of Irish Studies, University of Liverpool. She is author of *W.B. Yeats, the Abbey Theatre, Censorship, and the Irish State* and the forthcoming book *Revolutionary Lives: Constance and Casimir Markievicz*.

Marie Coleman is a lecturer in Modern Irish history in the School of History and Anthropology at the Queen's University of Belfast. She is author of a number of books on modern Irish history including *The Irish Revolution, 1916–1923* and *County Longford and the Irish Revolution, 1910–1923*.

Therese Caherty is a feminist and activist, co-convenor of the Feminist Open Forum and Chairperson of the Irish Women Workers' Union Commemoration Committee.

Angelina Cox, Lisa Connell and Jenni Garland are activists and members of the Rosie Hackett Bridge Campaign.

Catherine Ann Cullen is a graduate of the M.Phil in Creative Writing at Trinity College Dublin. Her work has been published in *The Doghouse Book of Ballad Poems*, *The Stinging Fly* and *College Green*. Her poetry collections are *A Bone in My Throat* and *Strange Familiar*.

Rosemary Cullen Owens taught Women's History in the Women's Studies Dept. in UCD from 1991–2012. Among her publications are *Smashing Times: A History of the Irish Women's Suffrage Movement, 1889–1922*; *Louie Bennett: A Biography* and *A Social History of Women in Ireland, 1870–1970*.

James Curry is a Digital Humanities Doctoral Scholar in Modern Irish History at the Moore Institute, NUI Galway, and author of *Artist of the Revolution: The Cartoons of Ernest Kavanagh.*

Francis Devine is a labour historian. He is a former editor of *Saothar*, the journal of the Irish Labour History Society, of which he is a past President. He is editor of *A Capital in Conflict: Dublin City and the 1913 Lockout.*

Elizabeth Gillis is a researcher and historian. She works in Kilmainham Gaol as a tour guide. She is the author of *The Fall of Dublin, Revolution in Dublin: A Photographic History 1913–23*, and *Women of the Irish Revolution: A Photographic History.*

Mary McAuliffe is an historian and lecturer in Women's Studies at UCD. Her books include *Kathleen Browne, 1876–1943: Patriot, Politician and Practical Farmer*, and *Fanny Taylor's Irish Homes and Irish Hearts*. She co-edited *Irish Feminisms: Past, Present and Future* and *Sexual Politics in Modern Ireland*. She is past President of the Women's History Association of Ireland (WHAI).

Ferghal McGarry is Senior Lecturer in History at Queen's University, Belfast. He is the author of a number of books on Irish history in the twentieth century, including *Frank Ryan, Irish Politics and the Spanish Civil War*; *The Rising: Easter 1916* and *The Abbey Rebels of 1916: A Lost Revolution.*

Gerri O'Neill is a historian currently completing her Ph.D on women and the Irish revolutionary period.

Padraig Yeates is a journalist, publicist and trade union activist. He is also author of several books including the acclaimed *Lockout: Dublin 1913*, *A City in Wartime*, *A City in Turmoil* and *A City in Revolution.*

INDEX